W9-CBM-097

HOW TO MAKE

$100,000

A YEAR

IN HOME
MAIL ORDER
BUSINESS

Barry Z. Masser

PRENTICE HALL
Englewood Cliffs, New Jersey 07632

Prentice-Hall International (UK) Limited, *London*
Prentice-Hall of Australia Pty. Limited, *Sydney*
Prentice-Hall Canada, Inc., *Toronto*
Prentice-Hall Hispanoamericana, S.A., *Mexico*
Prentice-Hall Of India Private Limited, *New Delhi*
Prentice-Hall of Japan, Inc., *Tokyo*
Simon & Schuster Asia Pte. Ltd., *Singapore*
Editora Prentice-Hall do Brasil, *Rio de Janeiro*

10 9 8 7 6 5 4 3

Library of Congress Cataloging-in-Publication Data

Masser, Barry Z.
How to make $100,000 a year in home mail order business / by Barry Z.
Masser.
    p. cm. Includes index.
    ISBN 0-13-397456-1 :
    1. Mail-order business—Handbooks, manuals, etc. I. Title.
HF5466.M35   1992
658.8'72—dc20   91-40187
                                                           CIP

ISBN 0-13-397456-1

PRENTICE HALL
Professional Publishing
Englewood Cliffs, NJ 07632
Simon & Schuster. A Paramount Communications Company

Printed in the United States of America

About the Author

Barry Z. Masser has served as advertising and Marketing director for several major corporations and is president of LeadFlow, Inc., a Seattle-based direct response firm. He is also a feature writer for Telemarketing Magazine and other marketing publications and a guest lecturer on advertising and marketing at leading universities.

Other Books by the Author

$36,000 a Year in Your Own Home Merchandising Business

Power-Selling by Telephone

The Corporate Caller-Skills Program

Complete Handbook of All-Purpose Telemarketing Scripts

HOW TO MAKE A $100,000 A YEAR IN HOME MAIL ORDER BUSINESS

Claim Your Share of $12 Billion in Annual Mail Order Sales Without Leaving Your Residence

By Barry Z. Masser

Introduction

1. UNDERSTANDING MAIL ORDER AND DECIDING HOW YOU WANT TO OPERATE

2. A REVEALING LOOK AT SOME OF THE WORLD'S RICHEST MAIL ORDER MARKETS

6. MAIL ORDER POWER-SELLING TACTICS

7. LIST BUILDING: THE VITAL CORNERSTONE OF *ANY* MAILING PROGRAM

8. AD AND MAILER FORMATS THAT COMMAND THE ATTENTION OF BUYERS

The president of a mail order clothing company said, "People love the anticipation, then the thrill of receiving that package holding their selection. Ordering by mail is simply more romantic than walking into a store and buying something off the shelf."

The operator of a hardware specialty direct marketing company said, "Many consumers believe that the products offered by mail are different, and better values, than those in stores. And they are often correct."

A mail order food specialty executive said, "I believe that convenience is the main issue. Getting into the car, fighting traffic, finding a parking place, and slogging through pushy, noisy crowds to reach a mall is more than many shoppers want to put up with."

Thanks to this strong consumer loyalty to buying by mail, *new mail order entrepreneurs can hit the jackpot today just as they did 10, 75, or 150 year ago.* In fact, the opportunities for locating and marketing winning products and services by mail are far more abundant today than in the past. There has *never* been a better time to prosper in direct marketing, and as a result, there is plenty of room for start-ups in this robust and expanding industry.

How You Can Become a Home-Based Mail Order Operator

Almost every category of adult American has achieved the dream of working at home and producing personal income that equals or exceeds the salaries earned by working for someone. For example,

- Women raising children are building important mail order companies in their spare time. Some of their experiences are related in later pages.

- According to the U.S. Department of Commerce, Bureau of the Census, the world population is aging, and older people often switch from traditional jobs to home-based businesses. Retired people can keep their living standards up to or *past* preretirement levels and have the time of their lives doing it.

Introduction

Mail Order: One of America's Oldest, Most Reliable Money-Making Businesses

In the early nineteenth century Americans flooded westward by wagon and railroad. These settlers adjusted to the rigors of life on the plains, but they sorely missed many basic necessities and almost all luxuries. General stores were often minimally stocked, and visits by wagon merchants were few and far between. Thus, the mail order industry was born. Sears, Roebuck's catalog offered the pioneers a veritable wonderland of products. Receiving even the most modest item by mail was an adventure in a settler's otherwise bleak existence.

Today, some 150 years later, the mail order phenomenon continues to surge, generating well over *$12 billion in annual sales*. That enormous wave of revenue is shared by firms ranging in size from mass mail merchandisers to one-person companies.

THIS HANDBOOK HAS BEEN PREPARED ESPECIALLY FOR THE SMALLER, START-UP MAIL ORDER OPERATOR WHO *DOESN'T* HAVE A DEEP BACKGROUND IN MARKETING OR A FORTUNE TO INVEST IN COSTLY ADS OR HUGE STOCKS OF MERCHANDISE.

Why People Spend Billions on Mail Order

Mail order growth has surged in spite of the fact that most consumers can drive to shopping centers in a few minutes. While they can see, feel, and smell the merchandise displayed in typical retail outlets, consumers *continue* to set order-by-mail records. Three mail order experts tell why they believe this is happening:

12. AVOIDING PITFALLS THAT CAN SLOW YOUR GROWTH

13. SETTING UP YOUR MAIL ORDER COMPANY AT HOME

End Notes

Index

- Moonlighters find mail order a perfect way to double and often triple their regular income.

Those people and thousands of others who run their own mail order firms never have to leave the comforts of home. A daily stroll to the mail box can yield scores of new orders worth hundreds or thousands of cash dollars. How do these people build lives virtually free of traffic jams and financial anxiety?

A man from Virginia said, "For eight years I worked at a home security company, then decided I had enough of making my boss rich. I left and put together a small mail-out catalog of home security devices. I doubled my income in six months working from my apartment."

This handbook shows you exactly how to put together your own nominally priced catalog, complete with professional-quality copy and illustrations. It describes other mailing formats that work for virtually any product or service you decide to promote. An Oregon woman did it this way:

One day I went food shopping and tried to find a specially shaped wooden spoon for my wok. They didn't carry the more unusual items, so I decided right then and there to start a mail order firm specializing in hard-to-find cooking and baking accessories. It's grown faster than I ever dreamed possible.

Where are the merchandise sources that enabled this entrepreneur to enter business? What buying techniques does she use to buy dozens of unusual kitchen items at the lowest wholesale prices? The answers are included in this handbook.

There are *thousands* of opportunities like those waiting to be effectively exploited by mail order entrepreneurs. Chapter 2 covers some of today's hottest markets and gives you the sources for finding hundreds more. The surface hasn't yet been scratched. By following *the established mail order operating guidelines* described in this handbook, you can reach the same success enjoyed by the people just quoted—at minimum risk.

You will also find that almost *anyone* of average capabilities can start and operate his or her own highly profitable mail order business. *No* special training or skills are needed. And contrary to popular belief, you *don't* have to be a copywriter or graphic designer to prosper in mail order.

There is a windfall of valuable information in this handbook for *going businesses* as well. Thousands of established firms can dramatically boost their sales and profits by simply adding mail order to their regular marketing programs. For example,

> A hobby shop owner in the Midwest realized that there was no force as powerful as the names of past buyers sitting uselessly in his files. A simple but cleverly constructed monthly bulletin to this dynamic list brings him a huge return on investment. Almost *any* retailer can easily tap the same gold mine if the steps provided in this handbook are followed.

How the Strategies in These Pages Can Help You Start And Operate a Thriving Mail Order Business

A young couple works fulltime selling specialty gifts through magazine ads. In their third year of operation, they gross a five-figure income. THEY USE THE CRUCIALLY IMPORTANT LIST-BUILDING STRATEGIES AND THE EXTRAORDINARY "DDB" SYSTEM DETAILED IN CHAPTER 5 OF THIS HANDBOOK.

A disabled engineer stays home and puts 25 hours a week into selling special woodworking tools by mail. HE USES ENVELOPE ADDRESSING TECHNIQUES THAT COMMAND BUYER ATTENTION. HIS MAILERS ARE READ WHILE MOST OTHERS ARE TOSSED. CHAPTER 8 PROVIDES THE SIMPLE HOW-TO'S.

Two executives teamed up to start a marketing newsletter. Subscriptions, solicited exclusively by mail order, soared to over 400 the first year. THIS PHENOMENAL GROWTH IS ATTRIBUTED TO THE "INFO-JAMMING" APPROACH, ALSO DESCRIBED IN CHAPTER 8.

FULFILLMENT RIDE-ALONGS add more than $23,000 to the gross mail order sales of a first-year operator who sends out an offering of vintage photo prints. THIS PROVEN BUSINESS-BUILDING TACTIC IS FULLY EXPLAINED IN CHAPTER 6.

CHAPTER 9 PROVIDES THE POINT-BY-POINT WORKINGS OF EIGHT EXTREMELY POWERFUL MAIL ORDER PROGRAMS. Each remarkable campaign provides a number of vital keys that could very well lead you to profitability in record time. Why bother inventing risky new methods when these tested and proven techniques can quickly be used to your tremendous advantage?

How to figure mail order profit margins . . . how to process and deliver orders promptly and economically . . . how to steer clear of the 11 common pitfalls that can damage the growth of a mail order company . . . how to evaluate the fascinating but perilous import/export markets. Those and many other critically important areas are laid out for you in language you'll immediately understand.

While the mail order business is not by any means easy, this handbook effectively cuts through the complexities. It frankly advises you what to do—and what not to do—to establish a mail order "machine" that can produce automatic income day and night while you stay at home. It covers the basics as well as the little-known but highly sophisticated merchandising strategies developed by some of America's most formidable mail order leaders.

Most important, this handbook has been prepared to give you the advice you'll need now *and* for years to come. As your business grows, you'll turn to these pages to find precisely the information you need to help you work out the best moves.

Barry Z. Masser

Acknowledgments

This book reflects the methods and pure savvy used by mail order operators who work on a smaller scale. They are entrepreneurs fighting to compete with industry giants. In most cases, they are contending in this exciting field with remarkable success.

Tom Power, senior editor at Prentice Hall, felt that operators of those young and growing direct marketing firms could provide the best possible advice to new entrepreneurs. He was right. In developing this handbook, *practical* information came from scores of people and sources. The vast majority of them are in home-based direct marketing businesses that they started with some ideas, a slim budget, and lots of desire.

Karen Keith gave me a veritable mountain of invaluable facts about direct marketing to companies. Catherine Bergart zeroed in on the kind of information a new venture like hers needed. Susan DeFrancia, a remarkably innovative and industrious entrepreneur, contributed generously. Scores of homebased independent merchandisers shared the tips they use to get results.

Bob Stone's classic book *Successful Direct Marketing Methods*, published by Crain Publishing Company in 1975, and the *Seattle Direct Marketing Association* provided an enormous pool of outstanding guidance. Bill Leeds, my former partner and my co-author on our best-selling book *Power-Selling by Telephone,* led the way with expertise about prospect development and follow-up methods.

All of us wish you, the reader and direct marketing entrepreneur, the greatest success in this exciting field.

CHAPTER 1

UNDERSTANDING MAIL ORDER AND DECIDING HOW YOU WANT TO OPERATE

Nothing is taken for granted in this handbook. It does not assume that you are familiar with even the most fundamental aspects of mail order and the inevitable pitfalls that accompany each aspect. For that reason, this chapter provides information that should be extremely useful in giving you a better grasp of how mail order works and in helping you with the exceedingly important basic planning.

First, we'll look at what kind of people this handbook is intended to assist.

WHO WILL GET THE MOST OUT OF THIS BOOK

If you are just getting started in the process of *considering* a mail order business of your own, this volume is ideal for you. It will take you, step by step, from your interest in the field to the implementation of your first mail order promotion. Then, beyond that initial money-making program, it will give you invaluable guidance in the ongoing conduct of your business.

These pages are equally useful to both individual entrepreneurs and small- to medium-sized companies that never used mail order on a serious basis.

While mail order has a notorious reputation as a costly and high-risk enterprise that sometimes hits the jackpot in a spectacular way, it will be demonstrated that a *very modest investment* can get a business rolling. Also, you will discover how sound business practices can virtually remove the risk but keep the jackpot potential a reality.

Therefore, at one extreme, the mail order approaches in this volume can be fruitful for individuals who have to operate on a strict budget. And it's a marvelous choice for those who prefer to avoid personal selling or public contact. It works for people who are confined to a certain neighborhood, and it makes great sense for the handicapped—or for *anyone* who wants to make money working at home.

At the other end of the pole, this handbook supplies the needed mail order know-how to those fortunate enough to have substantial money to invest in promotions, but not much prior experience in selling products and services by mail.

In any case, you *don't* need special training or background to make your new mail order business work. By following the steps in each chapter, you *will* reach your objectives without making serious errors.

We'll now define the main areas of mail order to help you pinpoint how you want to operate in this field.

A CRYSTAL-CLEAR DESCRIPTION OF MAIL ORDER

Mail order encompasses various approaches. Over the years, descriptions have been mixed and muddied, so when you discuss programs with somebody, you'll be far better off if you don't trust terms like "direct response" or "media advertising" to help you make your point. Instead, explain the *detailed means* of making sales to make sure you are understood.

That said, however, here are the labels we'll use:

Media Advertising

There are two interesting aspects in advertising. One is *display ads* placed in magazines, newspapers, and/or periodicals. Typically, display ads have to be large enough to picture and describe one or more products and deliver information about price and how to order. Buyer response can be via phone call or mail.

Direct response display ads should not be confused with the kind of display ads run by, say, department stores when they announce new summer styles. The latter ad is primarily meant to heighten consumer interest and increase sales *indirectly*. But most ads of that kind *do not* call for immediate consumer action as a mail order ad must do.

Mail order *classified ads* can endeavor to sell something in the space of a few tightly packed words, but they are used to much greater advantage in building a mailing list. A case in point is a mail order firm that offers a free catalog through a classified ad. People interested in the ad's stated product area will respond, thus becoming strong prospects.

Spot ads on radio or TV will plug a product or service and then ask for buyer response, usually via a toll-free 800 number. Certain broadcast channels in some markets, during other than prime-time slots, can still be priced comparatively low, as you will soon see.

Direct Response Catalog Distribution

When funds are limited, a mail order operator can *hand deliver* catalogs to consumer residences in a certain geographical area. *No* mailing or ad space expenses are entailed. Such modest beginnings have been known to blossom into robust enterprises.

Much more information is provided later both on the principal categories listed and on variations of those themes.

Starting your own mail order business is based on taking certain building steps in logical sequence. It works this way.

THE STEPS IN GETTING STARTED

The accompanying flowchart in Figure 1-1 shows the vital steps that have to be taken in starting a *direct mail* business. Eliminate "lists" and "mailing" for a catalog distribution promotion and other minor modifications for media advertising.

1.	Identify product/service		2.	Budget the program
3.	Allocate time		4.	Set up the business
5.	Set expectations		6.	Buy/warehouse
7.	Obtain lists		8.	Define offer
9.	Format		10.	Print
11.	Mail		12.	Fulfill orders
13.	Evaluate results		14.	Follow-up

Figure 1-1

You can see that the sequence of some early steps can be switched with others without negative impact on your overall program. For example, there would be no harm in allocating your personal time *before* you identify products. And it may very well be that budgeting your business might precede every other step and so forth. The sequence of steps 5 to 14 should *not* be changed, and *don't skip any steps since all are vital!*

Here's a quick guide on the specific chapters to reference when you need more facts on any of the steps.

HOW EACH CHAPTER WILL HELP YOU

A brief explanation of each step is now provided, along with guidance on where to look for further information on that step. While you are urged to read this *entire* handbook, the following quick-reference system may help you later if a question comes up.

Step 1: Identify Product or Service

Focus on at least a general family of products and/or services. Try to arrive at a choice you personally like or have above-average knowledge about. The more original the better, but your selection should still have either mass market appeal or strong pulling power in a specialized market. *Chapters 2 and 3* will help.

Step 2: Budget the Program

Once you know what kind of products you'll offer, figure out how much you'll be able to spend on product, printing, postage and other necessities. Continue reading *Chapter 1, then review Chapter 11.*

Step 3: Allocate Time

Work out a plan for how much time you'll be able to devote to your mail order operation. A big budget makes no sense if you won't have time to take care of incoming orders. Your available time will have a strong bearing on how ambitious your undertaking should be. *Chapter 12* may assist you in predicting how long it takes to get things done.

Step 4: Set Up the Business

Accounting, permits, any required licenses, and similar matters are now handled. See *Chapters 11 and 12.*

Step 5: Set Expectations

Based on your budget, your available time, and the estimated appeal of your chosen product or service, how many orders will you receive? It's *always* a rough guess in the beginning, but you must have some kind of figure to shoot for. Look at *Chapter 11.*

Step 6: Buy/Warehouse

Zero in on *specific* products that reside in your selected categories. Search for the best values—but in quantities that are based on your budget, your sales expectations, and storage facilities. Home-based operators have to be extremely careful about stock—unless products can be sent to buyers directly from the source (drop shipped). Read *Chapters 3, ll, 12, and 13.*

Step 7: Obtain Lists

For *direct mail* programs, the right lists are the very lifeblood of a solid mail order business. Read *Chapters 5, 6, and 7.*

Step 8: Define Offer

Create the appeal—or hire someone who can help you do it. The basic message you want to develop is; "Here's what we're selling . . . this is why it's a great value . . . and these are the things we'll do for you when you order." *Chapters 6, 9 and 10* are the places to go for this information.

Step 9: Format

Design your catalog, mailer, or ad. *Simple* is usually best. There are endless possibilities. *Chapter 8* has the most to say on this topic.

Step 10: Print

Selecting the right printer for your needs *will* save you money, grief, and time. See *Chapters 5, 8, 11, and 12.*

Step 11: Mail

In direct mail, you have a number of mailing options open to you. The type of program you plan will point logically to bulk rate, first class, or other method. Cost, speed, and image are determining factors. *Chapters 5 and 11* deal with mailing methods and costs.

Step 12: Fulfill Orders

One very good way to assure growth is by getting customer orders out fast and in good shape. You will find out that effective fulfillment goes a lot farther than simply boxing an order and mailing it out. *Chapters 9 and 11* tell the story.

Step 13: Evaluate Results

One expert put it beautifully: "If you can't measure results, *don't do it at all!*" There is no way to build a mail order business intelligently without knowing what kind of effort it takes to get certain results. *Refer to Chapter 11.*

Step 14: Follow-Up

Any successful mail order operator will tell you that more people will buy as they become familiar with your company. One-offer, one-time promotions are often futile in this business. *Chapter 9 is devoted to follow-up methods.*

Now a few observations about a home-based mail order enterprise.

OPERATING YOUR MAIL ORDER BUSINESS
FROM HOME

If there's a business of genuinely unlimited potential that can be conducted from your residence, it *is* mail order. Since buyers would never see your place of business under normal conditions, there are few sensitive or awkward aspects in working from home in mail order. The two areas that *can* present complexities are:

- Adequate space to store product inventory and necessary equipment safely.

- Using a home address, or a P.O. box number that can look sinister or unprofessional to some would-be buyers.

Both dilemmas can be solved neatly, so don't let those items put you off. Chapter 13 offers some excellent and proven solutions.

A home-based mail order operation also works nicely if your offer utilizes 800 inbound telephone lines. Some home entrepreneurs advertise 24-hour service and use voice mail to capture the incoming orders. You make money without leaving your favorite chair (except to empty the mailbox). Even your bank deposit can be mailed.

When a start-up venture can eliminate rent, utilities, parking expenses, and the other steep costs that accompany the setting up of an outside office—plus provide tax advantages—chances of success are enormously enhanced.

What can you figure on spending on a new mail order venture? We'll look at that question now.

WHAT KIND OF INVESTMENT IS REQUIRED?

Figures used here may differ widely from one part of the country to another, and since inflation marches inexorably on, the numbers are almost certain to grow.

A modest mailer to a small list (5,000) can run as little as $1,500. A catalog mailing would run considerably more due to larger printing costs, steeply higher postage, and the bigger bill for design and production.

When large mailings are done, incremental (cost per prospect) costs go down. It costs only marginally more money to print a far greater number of promotional pieces or catalogs. Therefore, you will realize much better economies by sending out bigger mailings, if you can budget more dollars.

Print and broadcast ads are usually the most expensive ways to generate buyers—and the most risky due to their unpredictability. There is one cable channel in an outlying Midwest market that will sell 30-second off-time spots for $250 each. Good deal, but who's watching? And don't forget the cost of creating and producing that spot.

Magazine and newspaper display advertisers find few bargains, particularly in the publications that are proven mail order winners. Frankly, this is *not* the way for small-budget mail order beginners to start.

So you *can* get off to a solid, professional start in mail order on a nominal cash outlay. You can and should cut corners sharply in some areas, but definitely *not* in others. By the time you complete this book, you'll know exactly where to cut and where not to.

GETTING STARTED ON A SHOESTRING

An Indiana woman had the grand sum of $225 to invest in a mail order business. She had come across a shipment of very nice desk lamps, comparable to $30 retail, that could be bought for $6 each. She typed out simple descriptive copy, reproduced a photo of the lamp that appeared on each box, and put together a one page mailer. Cost: $90.

Three neighborhood kids gladly earned $25 each to spend an afternoon distributing the bulletin to offices in Indianapolis. Total cash outlay to date: $165. Note: The lamp supplier generously agreed to sell her lamps *after* she sold them, so a volume purchase was not necessary.

Within the week, 43 lamps had sold at $15 each. The balance sold out on a following promotion 30-days later. Net profit; around $650. This amount financed exploration for new products, upgraded printing, and enabled wider distribution of what was now a four page product bulletin.

Practically *anybody* can build a mail order business with a very small cash start and then reinvest profits to gradually strengthen the enterprise. There are hundreds, maybe thousands, of success stories like that one.

We'll now survey some of the mail order markets and products that look extremely good now and for the future.

CHAPTER 2

A REVEALING LOOK AT SOME OF THE WORLD'S RICHEST MAIL ORDER MARKETS

Practically any product or service people use is a candidate for mail order. For that reason, this chapter highlights only a few of the vast markets open to you as a mail order operator. Specialties can be as finely targeted as reproductions of antique furniture hardware or as universally appealing as household cleaning supplies. Almost *nothing* can be excluded as a potential moneymaker. The possibilities are nothing less than staggering.

To help you gain insight into various healthy mail order markets, the following profiles might be of interest. If you are already certain about your products and markets, skip to Chapter 3.

EASILY THE HOTTEST MARKET UNTIL THE YEAR 2040

Top business experts are virtually unanimous in selecting the "baby boom" generation as the best bet for big mail order sales through at least the next 40 years. Here are some startling facts:

There are *76 million* postwar baby boomers in America and only heaven knows how many worldwide. This enormous chunk of humanity, born between 1946 and 1964, sets the course of trends. They create industries and make new billionaires as they march through the years.

In the 1950s, boomers consumed diapers, toys and baby food in prodigious quantities. Fast-food enterprises thrived in the 1960s thanks to them. Fashion took off as this force turned teen in the 1970s. The 1980s saw boomers take interest in health and fitness, and that triggered the making of fortunes in businesses offering weight loss and vitality.

Since the beginning of time, the most effective sellers have been successful in guessing where population trends would head. One nationally known mail order clothing firm started the 1970s at $600,000 in annual sales and soared to *$99 million* just a few years later. They correctly predicted the emerging rage for fashion and made a fortune in selling the denim look.

From now until the year 2040, the aging boomer population is expected to buy products and services that promise a more youthful look. Solutions to baldness, wrinkles, and other appearance deficits will undoubtedly produce a new and large group of wealthy marketers, many of them selling boomers by mail.

While there are scores of solid choices as to the products and services that will sell to the tidal wave of baby boomers, a very strong area is money-making opportunities. As this huge population segment starts to leave traditional job markets, they will turn to methods of making money in home businesses. If you offer them ways to earn at home, you will almost certainly be poised to build a profitable mail order company for yourself.

Next, consider this aspect of mail order potential. It's very nearly as dynamic as maturing people.

INCREDIBLE MAIL ORDER OPPORTUNITIES FOR ESTABLISHED BUSINESSES

In one northern U.S. city, two major carpet stores serve the area's 400,000 inhabitants. One regularly sends out promotions to its customers and prospects. The other relies almost entirely on newspaper ads and TV spots to get new buyers into the store. The former retailer profits far more by ringing up about *$220,000 more in annual* *sales* than its chief rival. Most of that extra business can be attributed *directly* to the bimonthly mailings.

Why established companies neglect their old customers is a profound mystery. Practically *every* business operator knows that the most fruitful list available consists of *past buyers*. That fact will be stressed often in these pages.

If you have made a purchase at a certain store—and whatever you bought worked out to your satisfaction—wouldn't you be apt to respond to a new offer from that source? Of course. Based on hard facts, old customers are about 40 percent more likely to buy than are new prospects who probably are not acquainted with the firm making the offer.

Golden opportunities to profit through mail order are available to retailers, manufacturers, distributors, and service firms of all descriptions. In fact, virtually *any* going company can significantly increase sales by mailing. Even restaurants and service stations stand to gain in a big way by contacting past customers.

Amazingly, lots of firms never make any effort to capture the names of buyers. Building that database is the first step in establishing a mail order program. One home electronics retail chain asks *every* retail buyer for name and address—even if the purchase totals only a few dollars. Its seasonal catalog goes out to millions of consumers and does many millions of dollars in business.

More about catalog sales later. Right now, we'll take a look at the ever-expanding specialty merchandise market.

HIGH-IMPULSE SPECIALTY MERCHANDISE IS SOLD BY THE TON

Mass market specialty merchandise is, very frankly, junk. This fabulously profitable but somewhat risky mail order category includes the high-impulse items we are constantly exposed to on display racks strategically placed near the checkout lines at markets. These products are cute, colorful, and priced so our decision to buy is driven by emotion instead of common sense. Specialty merchandise encompasses novelty key chains, miniflashlights, outrageous combs, oversized plastic paperclips in dayglo colors, and literally thousands of other items of that nature we buy almost unconsciously.

Most of us enjoy making these purchases, and perhaps even get some use out of these novelties before they fail or grow stale. The real point is; they sell in astounding volume in stores and by mail order. High-impulse items arrive at U.S. ports by the millions, and countless merchants buy them by the gross. Consumers never seem to get tired of specialty merchandise; it's an area that's been going strong since wagons carried it across the Wild West.

At least four West Coast companies import specialty merchandise from the Far East and sell millions of dollars worth of the stuff to an army of independent distributors who, in turn, conduct their own mailing campaigns to the ultimate consumer. Hundreds of smaller-scale buyers do their own importing and marketing. Some serious drawbacks in becoming a specialty merchandise importer are the following:

- Doing business with overseas factories is a tricky game. If a shipment is the wrong size or color, little recourse is available to the buyer. Most transactions are cash in advance.

- Almost *every* shipment includes defective items. The buyer almost always has to absorb the loss.

- The time between order and delivery can easily turn into months. So buying for seasonal sales is exceedingly risky.

For a mail order operator, the keys are large volume sales and hefty profit margins. But it *is* a good product category if the pitfalls can be avoided. You'll learn more about specialty merchandise mail order operations later.

The next mail order category we'll survey is related closely to specialty merchandise, but is a rung higher on the quality ladder.

GIFT SALES BY CATALOG ARE SOARING

High-impulse specialty merchandise satisfies a consumer's need to sometimes be frivolous and blow a few dollars. This characteristic also holds true for gift items that reside at the low end of the price scale. But the gift category is massive since it covers items that retail for thousands of dollars per item. While the gift category definitely includes things we buy for ourselves, it really describes items suited for giving.

Gifts encompass glassware, decorative accessories, jewelry items, and any other product one would purchase for another person.

Since gifts do cover such a vast price spectrum, a mail order company is well advised to zero in on a certain position in the overall market. You can't very well offer a $9.95 plastic clock and show it next to an imported $300 hand-crafted bronze mantle clock. There are healthy markets for low-, medium-, and high-priced gifts, but one company can't effectively handle all through one catalog.

A notably successful gift seller put it this way:

"There was never a doubt in my mind about the kinds of gifts I wanted to sell. When I planned my business, I knew I wanted to handle better ornamental glass pieces. These are hand-blown items, all originals.

"I could sell hundreds of cheaper pieces that make perfectly nice gifts, but I was determined to build my image around better quality and higher prices for customers who want to give something special."

During good times and bad, gifts will sell. Every special occasion brings new demand. Birthdays, graduations, anniversaries, and holidays never stop. Companies give gifts to employees, so direct mail to businesses is one more area that can be *extremely* profitable.

A close cousin to gift sales is the fashion market.

FASHION ITEMS AND HOME-CRAFTED WARES CAN SELL FAST, IN HUGE QUANTITIES

Trendy products are tricky mail order products. They hold the potential for enormous profits or steep losses. Fads emerge suddenly and create firestorms of demand that strip shelves and warehouses of every available product. The same volatility can cause demand to vanish without warning, leaving every merchant holding worthless inventory. The most successful mail order operators try to offer fashions that steer away from the exotic.

This conservative approach is particularly important in cases where a catalog is mailed that might remain in a customer's hands for a period of many months.

Land's End, L. L. Bean, Inc., and Spiegels are three clear catalog clothing leaders, to name just a few. All offer a wide range of clothing items that always seem to appeal to their respective customers. The most obvious adjustments in selection from one catalog to the next are those reflecting the changing seasons. Styles are definitely mainstream.

Smaller operators are wise to stick with fashion accessories due to the warehousing demands in stocking hundreds of clothing items in a variety of sizes. Yet some smaller-scale mail order leaders have found success in offering a narrow choice of clothing items, for example, just jeans, exclusively two-piece bathing suits, and so forth. One outfit found prosperity in marketing strictly women's size 9. At least one other confines its selection to very large sizes.

Thousands of people who make products on home sewing machines dream of building businesses around their wares. Susan DiFino is one home manufacturer who made her dreams a reality:

> Susan made up a set of sample garters and mailed them, along with prices and available color options, to the accessory buyer of a major national fashion retailer. About two weeks later, she had an order for *8,000 pieces.*

> Ms. DiFino eventually had to invest in an industrial sewing machine and other high-volume equipment that barely fit in a spare bedroom. Then she had to hire and train assistants. But the job got done, and Susan is producing thousands of garters every month. *All* business is done by mail in her residence.

We'll switch now to a mail order market that probably will *never* lose steam.

EDUCATION IS A LEADER IN DOLLAR VOLUME AND PROFITS

Education is a wide-ranging field. It includes correspondence courses, subliminal tapes (with hidden motivational messages), weight loss programs, and books on tape. That's only the tip of the iceberg.

Our increasingly technological society is fast creating the necessity to learn more. Keeping one's head above water demands the acquisition of new skills. And the pressures of competing have spawned new markets for books and tapes on keeping it together emotionally.

Baby boomers, discussed earlier, are buying record numbers of programs for retaining youth. Remember, that particular market of 76 million men and women will be dynamite until about the year 2040.

People by the millions will be looking for ways to escape the hectic routine of getting to work and back. They will be searching for home business opportunities. That means retraining on a colossal scale. Estimates tell us that 10 percent of the American population will work at home by the year 2000. Each of those individuals will have to learn how to do it. Promotions to both consumers and businesses are, and will continue to be, fruitful.

Companies are constantly seeking the how-to's on sales, computer operations, videotaping, customer service, and *scores* of other topics pertinent to more efficient management. There is virtually no end to the possibilities.

How can a small independent mail order operator cash in on the information boom? Here's just one example:

> A retired engineer in Chicago put together a mail order catalog filled with course titles that had been discontinued by their original publishers. He has the programs updated, and then markets them to a list of 4,000 small- to medium-sized corporations. Annual volume in his third year of operation is $180,000 and growing fast.
>
> The former publishers help in any way they can since they are once again earning money on programs they long considered dead.

Education is a winner. It's a needed service and a *proven* moneymaker in mail order.

Speaking of business, here's another product category that always sells well.

OFFICE SUPPLIES THAT ALWAYS ATTRACT BUYERS

Do you personally know of a business, however small, that does not use a computer? Every firm that does even a little accounting uses up computer paper, printer supplies, and diskettes. Plus, they buy software and books on how to use the new programs. Add to that the countless hundreds of other items consumed in almost every office. Standard business forms, like employment applications and time sheets, are also heavily used. Demand is *always* present.

When a firm needs supplies, that need is generally now, *today*. Many companies don't usually order small supplies in advance, and trips to the local retailer are often inconvenient. Therefore, when a mailer on these popular office supplies is sent out to companies, it's a virtual certainty that some will be in a state of immediate need and will order. Then, if your service is good, prices are competitive, and product quality is acceptable, that firm will buy repeatedly from your follow-up product bulletins.

A San Diego woman lost her aerospace job after 16 years and chose to start a small mail order office supply business:

> "I concentrated on computer supplies. My first mailer was a simple four-page piece with photographs supplied by various manufacturers. With the pictures, I included a little copy and retail prices. A separate order form was enclosed in the envelope. I could only afford to mail to 700 companies, but I got 26 orders totaling almost $900. It was a very encouraging start.

> "The modest profit paid for the next mailing, and I was on the way. That was two years ago. Now I'm working on a 16-page mailer with 135 items. My income is almost double what it was after 16 years on the same job with a big company."

Since waves of the future are often tied closely to big money in mail order, riding the computer surge seems like a safe bet for many years to come.

Let's go back once again to that pace-setting baby boom generation and their fierce grasp on eternal youth and health.

FOOD SUPPLEMENT MARKETERS
CAN MAKE FORTUNES

A friend told me this story recently. It nicely sums up the success that is often achieved in the mail order food supplement business:

> "When I was around 13, I remember going with a friend to his father's place of business. In one little room, the man had a couple of machines that he used to make some kind of vitamin capsules. There were no other employees that I recall, and he did all the work himself. These people weren't wealthy. In fact, they lived very modestly.

> "A few years later, this vitamin maker switched from selling to retailers and started using mail order. He placed small ads in the weekend newspaper, offering his product direct to consumers. In no time, my friend's father had around 30 employees and one

entire floor of a new commercial building. Before long, he had around 150 different nutrition products and sold them nationally. The business has been growing ever since."

Any user of vitamins, food supplements, and other health-oriented products can buy anything he or she needs simply by strolling to the nearest drugstore. Yet untold thousands of people spend record amounts of money buying essentially the same items through the mail. One of the biggest food supplement marketers, based in Illinois, regularly buys the entire back page of one of America's leading syndicated newspaper magazines. That's a full color ad, and very expensive. You can be certain the cash returns are consistently handsome.

There are definitely some complexities in food supplement selling, particularly with respect to requirements imposed by the Food and Drug Administration (FDA), plus possible state regulations. It's also an intensely competitive business where consumer trust is an absolute basic. The products themselves can be obtained from manufacturers who will private label. More about that interesting topic later.

Despite the drawbacks, it's a good bet that vitamins, skin creams, special hair preparations, and all the other products in that family will continue to sell briskly for the foreseeable future thanks to that baby boomer wave.

If you have a pastime you love, the next area might be especially interesting to you.

THE HOBBY MARKET IS PURE DYNAMITE

People will have more time for themselves as the years pass, and strong mail order businesses are built on the spare-time passions of individuals all over the world. For example,

- Dozens of mail suppliers offer hard-to-find parts for old firearms. Gun collectors everywhere anxiously await each new mailing.

- Coin and stamp collectors constantly search for new additions to their collections. They shop at shows and scour the pages of mailers for new finds.

- Most professional and amateur artists count on receiving bulletins and catalogs packed with hundreds of everyday and exotic supplies, from airbrush nozzles to Japanese clay forming tools.

There is seemingly no end to the special interests people develop. When a person does get involved in a hobby, it usually becomes something of an obsession, one that absorbs large blocks of time and often far more money than he or she should spend on it.

These hobbyists actively *seek* sources for the components they need. Big mail order businesses have been built on tiny classified ads that offer a free catalog. Through such a modest start, mailing lists of enthusiasts can be quickly established. More often than not, the operator of a hobby-oriented mail order business is himself or herself an aficionado in that field. Therefore, if you are deeply absorbed in some area of interest, you can be certain that millions of other people are, too. And there is *no* reason why they wouldn't buy from you.

To this point, we've concentrated on various *product* categories that work successfully in mail order programs. Now we will take a look at a sampling of *service* ideas.

HOW SERVICES ARE SOLD SUCCESSFULLY BY MAIL

Big mail order sales are chalked up by a renowned astrologer who will do a buyer's chart when certain facts like date, time, and place of birth are provided.

A graphologist asks customers to send a page of longhand so handwriting analysis can be done. Promotional material describes how many corporations use this type of analysis to peg a job applicant's key personality characteristics.

For a larger fee, one company in a northern state will research and draw up your family tree. The color illustration makes a beautiful addition to any photo album or mantle.

Related to the family tree idea is a search for one's coat of arms. A buyer's last name, plus a few other basic facts, supposedly enables this outfit to come up with the same embellishment your distant ancestors carried on their shields. If a family's early history was in northern Europe, this task can be accomplished more readily.

Several enterprising firms can supply a reprint of the newspaper front page that was published on the day you were born. This has been popular for years.

There are even a few mail order entrepreneurs who claim the ability to do a psychic reading on any individual who sends along some old item they once carried like a house key or ballpoint pen. While that may seem rather close to the ethical line, it does demonstrate the fact that almost nothing is too bizarre.

Some of these concepts require special knowledge. Others take research time. All of them enjoy the leading attribute of any service offer: little or no inventory is needed. Another thing is, each one appeals strongly to the buyer's ego. It is simply human nature for us to seek more information about who and what we are, and where we've been and where we're going.

Here's another interesting wrinkle on profitably marketing services by mail order.

USING 900 LINES TO EARN EXTRA MAIL ORDER REVENUE

One East Coast company specializes in locating and selling hard-to-find crystal, stemware, sterling, flatware, and china place settings. Consumers looking for a saucer, a soup spoon, a plate, or other replacement items call this firm's 900 number to find out if the desired piece is available.

The 900 number enables this mail order company to charge $1.25 per minute for each inquiry call, whether the correct item is located or not. This firm also purchases pieces of value, and 900 calls are often placed by people anxious to find out how much their items are worth. Tiny display ads attract a high volume of calls from consumers interested in both buying and selling.

Income from call-ins can amount to substantial dollars *over and above* the income generated through selling replacement items. An increasing number of companies that deal in *information* are looking at 900 telephone service to boost income. They are concluding that it makes good sense to charge for their expertise or advice on where to find certain elusive items. The individual seeking a serving piece in a long-extinct or rare pattern is just one example of many where specialized information is worth cash.

More information on how 900 telephone service works appears in Chapter 4. One final word about the immense potential in mail order.

BILLIONS OF DOLLARS IN EMERGING OVERSEAS MARKETS

Developing countries all over the world will eventually become prime customers for U.S. marketers. It is probable that growing affluence in distant lands will create a flood of prospects for goods we may take for granted in America.

These changes will evolve slowly. Aside from many as yet unanswered questions about the economic conditions in new democracies, there are major uncertainties regarding the limitations that may be imposed on foreign sellers.

Also, before *any* mail order marketing can be considered in a developing economy, local publications and consumer mailing lists have to exist. So there's a long way to go, but these far-away markets are definitely one more future possibility of immense potential in the mail order field.

At this point, small and large mail order merchants alike should keep in touch with the progress in new free market economies. The situation today is not unlike the highly speculative environment in early America, where mail order pioneers like Sears were often big winners.

Now, some guidance on how to buy like a pro.

CHAPTER 3

WHERE AND HOW BIG-INCOME OPERATORS GET THE HOTTEST-SELLING PRODUCTS

This chapter is about *how to avoid being a sucker* when you purchase products for your mail order business. You *don't* need decades of experience to buy smart. By avoiding some common pitfalls—and proceeding with proven practices—you can give your business *every possible advantage.*

Along with sound advice on where to check for excellent buys, you'll find tips on where *not* to shop for mail order products.

A CRASH COURSE ON HOW THE SMARTEST BUYERS WORK

Harvey Freeland has the awesome responsibility of locating, negotiating, and buying more than 1,250 different products for a mail order firm that does over $10 million in annual sales. He seems to function by intuition and pure magic to the average observer. When Harvey sorts through a huge pile of wristwatches and comes up with one he feels is a winner, one wonders how that particular choice is made when it is virtually identical to scores of others in the small mountain of watches on his desk. This top buyer chuckles when untrained observers wonder at his skill.

> "Just about anybody can do what I do, as long as certain guidelines are followed. When I stick to those basic rules of buying, the 'right products' kind of pop out of the samples I'm looking at. But even then, I'll make mistakes here and there. Not everything sells as well as I feel it should. You have to be ready for disappointments in this business."

Harvey finds products through an array of sources, including:

- Agents representing overseas manufacturers.
- U.S. firms
- Occasional trips to the Far East and Europe
- Companies anxious to unload surplus items
- Start-up marketers attempting to establish distribution

And others. Some are strong potential sources, some are not. But on almost any weekday, this busy buyer can expect dozens of samples to cross his desk. He screens almost every one in his constant search for the few items that will be bought and eventually presented to the firm's huge customer base via catalogs and mailers.

Two extremely important pieces of advice from Harvey Freeland are now offered. One has to do with buying *as close to the manufacturer as you possibly can.* The other pertains to certain suppliers that rarely if ever offer viable values to mail order operators, in spite of their claims to the contrary.

WHERE NOT TO BUY

When *any* mail order operator understands how basic product distribution works, there is much less chance of falling into the trap of paying too much for products.

Figure 3-1 pictures only one of many possible distribution systems. Regardless of minor variations that may actually exist in the case of a particular product, the real point is this:

THE LOWER DOWN THE SCALE A BUYER NEGOTIATES, THE HIGHER THE PRICE WILL BE AND THE LESS CONTROL THE BUYER CAN EXERCISE.

Figure 3-1—A Sample Distribution System

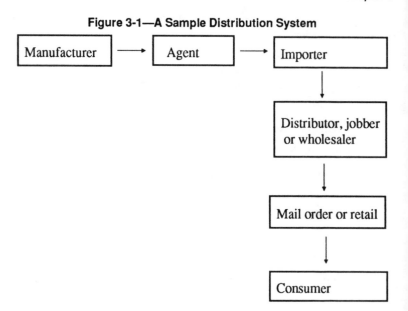

An overwhelming majority of overseas manufacturers are not geared up to handle their own marketing or exporting, so they often use agents who travel extensively on behalf of their clients.

Agents look for importers. These importers may also be distributors/jobbers/wholesalers. In fact, some retailers deal directly with agents if those stores purchase exceptionally large quantities of merchandise.

The ultimate consumer is always last in line. After all the profits have been tacked onto the cost of an item, it becomes available on a store counter or through mail order.

Again, each level has to add profit margin. So the per item price to *you* grows as it moves from the manufacturer down to the ultimate consumer. In the example of a distribution system given, a key chain that costs 8 cents to make could easily sell at $1.75 or much more at retail.

When bargains *are* available at a level as low as retail, it's usually because the merchandise is slow selling or distressed in some other way and the store wants to recover at least some cash on a bad decision. The problem is, once the product is gone, it can't be replaced. So it's of dubious value in a catalog or a large-scale mailer.

Moving up a notch on the scale to distributors, jobbers, and wholesalers, we have a situation where these terms are used very loosely. Whichever of the three words a particular firm uses to describe itself, your objective as a buyer is to find out exactly how many others have sold the merchandise prior to this level. The deal offered to you may sound good, but if your competitors have succeeded in purchasing the items at a level closer to the manufacturer, you'll be forced to sell at a higher price in order to profit.

Harvey Freeland points out one other interesting fact mail order buyers should know about the distribution system.

A few large and prospering U.S. companies import merchandise and resell it to very small companies and individuals who are led to believe they are buying the items at competitive prices. In some of these cases, the prices charged by these importers are not nearly low enough to allow competitive retail pricing. In fact, some aspiring mail order operators are paying the same or higher prices as those paid by the retailer.

In essence, these promoters *are* importers, but they charge much higher prices than they could charge.

In addition to importing gift merchandise and reselling it to small firms, companies in that category generally offer courses and other instructions on how to sell the gift items. While a few people do manage to sell products and achieve a degree of success through hard work, they are swimming upstream due to the unfavorable pricing offered by the slick operators.

While Harvey Freeland buys merchandise in 43 different product categories, he stresses the importance of *focusing* when doing the purchasing for a new mail order company.

THE ADVANTAGES OF NARROWING
YOUR PRODUCT SELECTION

One of the most frustrating dilemmas to any new mail order entrepreneur is *where to draw the line in terms of product selection.* A catalog showing some 600 products is nearly irresistible, and it's only natural that the owner of a start-up mail order company wants to debut with an effort of that magnitude. But the realities are usually guided by finite funds and space.

When planning the initial purchases for a new mail order enterprise, exceptional self-discipline has to be summoned in order to reach the following goals:

- It is infinitely better to offer more depth in fewer product categories. That means that you are likely to sell more if you show a rich selection of radios alone instead of a sparse choice of radios plus the introduction of another product category that's equally thin.

- If you are faced with an overwhelming selection of available radios, consider choosing an assortment of low-, medium-, and higher-priced models so you can appeal to a variety of consumer budgets and needs.

- When you *are* in a position to offer several product categories via mail order, select *related* products. As a case in point, the Indiana woman discussed earlier started with specially purchased desklamps. When she was able to expand her operation, business desktop accessories were added. Hence, there was a definite merchandise strategy apparent in her mailings because she could effectively target the kind of markets that might respond to *any* of her products. Obviously, toys would have been a poor choice in this instance.

- Which category should you start with? Select the one you know the most about or the one where you can get spectacular value. Economics *can* have more weight than emotion or knowledge if the good prices help you clinch success. You can grow to love almost anything that makes money for you.

You *don't* need a dazzling assortment of categories and items to make it in mail order. How many appealing single-item offers do you receive? Probably lots of them. If your selection is small in the initial stages, you can still sell effectively by media ads or mailers. A catalog may have to wait until later.

One more vital point will also be mentioned later in this handbook: In just about *any* successful mail order program, *a follow-up product or products are ready to send out to buyers.* The mail order vitamin company we talked about earlier does this masterfully. When consumers order products from this firm through its media ads, the firm sends *additional product flyers* along with the requested products and has regular catalog mailings.

We'll now explore the issue of how pricing is perceived by seasoned mail order buying pros.

WHY MORE FORTUNES ARE MADE THROUGH BUYING AND NOT SELLING

Nearly every major buyer agrees to this fascinating theory:

> Consumers who tend to purchase by mail are *not* as sensitive to price as shoppers who prefer stores. As a result, mail order companies that cut their selling prices can seriously impair their shot at prosperity.

If that is true—and there is little reason to doubt it—your mail order offer can safely carry prices equal to or even higher than retail stores. In fact, as you will discover later, mail order prices *have to be* set at substantial levels.

That means money is really made on buying, not selling. If a grandfather clock kit you offer is a solid $69 retail seller, you'll price it at $69 to $79 in your mailer or ad. But if you can buy those kits for $18 each instead of $24, *that's* where the profit is.

If you succeed in negotiating an $18 price for the clock kits, reducing your selling price to $59 in the hopes of selling a few more is absolutely futile. Most mail order shoppers simply *will not* recognize the difference! Unless a product is a household item, sold almost everywhere in huge quantities, a small percentage difference in price will mean nothing.

"Passing the savings on to the consumer" is rhetoric often thrown around by various merchants. The ones who actually do it are either misguided as to the real impact on most consumers or use that language purely as a promotional gimmick.

By all means, force yourself to see the exceptional buys you occasionally come across as opportunities for profit windfalls. Avoid rushing to hand the fatter margin over to your customers who won't notice the difference.

It's time to examine more fully the very important business of buying techniques.

WINNING NEGOTIATING TACTICS USED BY TOP PROS

Most people's eyes glaze when they hear the word "negotiate." It evokes images of confrontation, price manipulation, haggling over pennies and terms, and even outright hostility. Unfortunately, these unpleasant situations occur as often as not in buying, and they don't work to anyone's benefit.

Compare that disagreeable state of affairs to this comment from Ben Carlson, executive vice president of Vernay Laboratories and a quality control specialist:

> "... suppliers can no longer be played off one another for lower prices. They become your partners, and you have to help them improve so they can give you continually improving supplies for lower prices."

Business leaders like Ben Carlson believe that when a buyer succeeds in "winning" a contest over price, terms, quantity, or other major purchasing issue, the supplier will, from that point on, try to even up the score. That product source feels there is no loyalty, that the buyer will probably end up dealing with a competitor anyway, so why *not* try to recover the prior concession? Not much of a relationship!

In truth, any self-respecting supplier constantly seeks improvement. The very best information on what the market wants comes from retailers and mail order companies. *Your sources will listen if you take the time to communicate.* Tell them what you need to do business and most vendors will make an effort to fulfil your wishes. They want sales as much as you do.

We *are* moving strongly toward a national mood of cultivating better business relationships, and one of the relationships that needs lots of work is the buyer/seller partnership. When it's a trusting, mutually supportive hook-up, more gets done, quality and value increase, and work becomes much more fun. Today's best buyers *avoid* the old-fashioned haggling approach and practice instead the building of strong partnerships.

Building relationships with various product vendors does *not* mean a buyer caves in on prices or sheepishly goes along with every quoted aspect of a purchase proposal. It *does* mean taking an approach like the following one:

- First, positively identify the products you want to offer, right down to the nitty-gritty details like target prices, size, color, level of quality, the quantity you'll need, and so forth (see the *"Buying Checklist"* at the end of this chapter).

- Now list the sources that might carry the items you're looking for. Local suppliers should be telephoned to verify product availability and distant sources can be checked out by letter. (Sample letters are provided later.)

- Set appointments to visit sources that look like good possibilities. That's the professional way to operate.

- When you sit down with a seller, describe your business and its mission; then explain what items you're interested in. Get a quote *before* you reveal the target price you formulated earlier. When the vendor has a complete picture of your objectives, much more support can normally be expected. That's an important piece of the partnership philosophy.

During the course of your visit, do your best to get answers to *all* the questions on your "Buying Checklist."

- If there are serious differences between your target prices, needed quantities, or other crucial factors, politely explain these to the seller's representative.

 The fact that you initially stated your mail order objectives may help enormously since the seller isn't as likely to believe you are trying to improve the deal just for the sake of haggling. Instead, you are sincerely attempting to meet preset business goals.

The foregoing is a high-level business approach. It is negotiating respectfully but effectively.

Small and start-up mail order firms will inevitably encounter large suppliers accustomed to dealing in high-volume orders. Some may view your requirements with something resembling disdain. Here's how smaller operators can overcome that problem.

MAKING FAVORABLE ARRANGEMENTS
WITH LARGE SUPPLIERS

Some vendors look askance at any order that requires them to break a master carton that might hold many thousands of items. Or they may balk if your order is under a certain dollar amount, which can be a budget-buster to a fledgling mail order operator. Some suppliers are set up to ship massive quantities to big retail chains and mammoth mail order companies, and they really don't want to process small merchandise requests.

The following advice does *not* give you any secrets that will change the fundamental policies of those high-rollers, but it does provide an approach that *has worked* to give small mail order firms a foothold with high-volume sources.

Large-scale suppliers *are* acutely aware of the fact that many mail order enterprises grow fast. Today's little buyer might very well become a mass merchandiser down the road. It occurs regularly. So the way to deal with the giants is to let them know you are in business for the long haul, and their cooperation will *not* be forgotten when you orders reach major proportions.

Before we get into the specifics of the approach, here's a word about what *your* expectations in this situation should be:

- If a major supplier *does* agree to bend its policy and sell you a smaller quantity of goods, *don't* expect the same prices enjoyed by a national store chain. At the same time, avoid getting excited about a prohibitively high figure just because the company sees fit to do business with you. Good value *still has to be there*. Remember, the underlying objective in dealing with a big supplier is decent quality and competitive prices.

- You may also find it necessary to concede other advantages that normally go to big buyers. Items such as payment terms and delivery turnaround time may not be as favorable if you buy lower quantities. This is not intentional harassment, but a simple matter of big-dollar transactions commanding top priority.

One more tip: In the beginning of this relationship, avoid making other special requests of a firm that is already adjusting its procedures to accommodate you. Still, you should get what is coming to you and refuse to make sacrifices that could compromise your program.

The strongest points you can make when you talk to a representative of a big supplier are the following:

"While I fully realize that I'm asking you to sell me quantities that fall short of your firm's minimums, I'm planning energetic and sustained promotions of your products."

"I believe my company can rapidly become one of your valued customers. We don't expect to remain at current product need levels. When we *do* reach the status of a big buyer, you can count on our continued loyalty."

When it is more practical to communicate this message by mail, the following letters may be helpful to you.

SAMPLE LETTERS TO PRODUCT SUPPLIERS

When a company succeeds in identifying the best sources for its product and service needs, success comes a big step closer.

Based on a survey of 77 mail order firms and retailers, 86 percent of them constantly search for new sources for aiding expansion. At the same time, they never stop working to improve their dealings with their existing suppliers.

A manufacturer of fashion craft items constantly looks for new patterns and better deals on everything from thread to small sewing machines. She enjoys a never-ending inflow of exceptional values, superior quality, and innovative new looks and ideas. This mail order firm remains a step ahead of bigger competitors in selection, while prices are sharply competitive.

Here's how it's done. The following brief letter goes out to *every* potential supplier:

Attention: Customer Service,
        (Potential supplier's company name)

Enclosed is a photocopy of a (lace applique).

We are seeking a wholesale source that can supply this item. Current needs are 6,000 pieces, which should cover us for approximately the next 60 to 90 days.

Do you carry this item? Or have anything comparable to it? If not, we would appreciate your referring us to a source that might carry a similar item.

Thank you for your service.

Sincerely,

_____

        or

Dear ?:

Enclosed are swatches of several fabric patterns we use in our mail order promotions to home craft shoppers. We would like to know if you can supply these and, if so, how much they would cost per yard.

Also, we will be needing blue lace and would be interested in seeing anything you might have.

If these items are not in your line, we would be grateful for any advice you can provide on who we can contact in the industry.

Thanks for your service.

Sincerely,

_____

About one-fourth of these query letters attract an answer. Half of the responding suppliers do not carry the requested item, but provide valuable information on related products that may eventually be needed.

Next, consider the letter this mail order company uses to negotiate small quantities and good prices with the sources that respond to the above letter but require much larger purchases than the inquiring firm is prepared to buy:

Dear ?:

The applique sample you kindly mailed looks like it would ideally serve our needs for a mailer we're getting ready to introduce our spring line.

We realize you require a minimum order of 18,000 pieces, and certainly understand your position since we've been through similar situations with many of our other major suppliers. Most of them agreed to work with us on smaller initial orders than they normally like to handle, and we quickly reached and passed their minimums.

We really need your support now. If we can get that from you, you'll have a steady stream of business that should exceed your minimums quickly.

If you can work with us on 6,000 pieces, we can give you the order by return mail.

We deeply appreciate your special consideration and thank you in advance for assisting us in adding your fine product to our new mailing.

Sincerely,

———————————

When the supplier agrees to ship the smaller quantity, a letter like this serves to close the transaction:

Dear ?:

Per your approval letter of June 16, the following is our purchase order for 6,000 appliques. Please match the color indicated on the enclosed swatch.

We appreciate immediate shipment on your standard billing arrangements. Trade references are enclosed. These should facilitate prompt delivery. If you have any questions about these, please call me.

Again, we deeply appreciate your special consideration and look forward to a long and mutually beneficial business relationship with your company.

Sincerely,

———————————

For more vital information about buying, read the rest of this chapter.

A WORD ABOUT QUALITY

For the long-range, it doesn't pay to be in the business of selling junk. Much of the world has experienced decades of plastic toys that fall apart in your hands, electrical devices that blow fuses, and untold tons of other shoddy goods that invariably end up in the dumpster. Generally speaking, consumers have grown sick of wasting their money, and that trend is definitely picking up steam.

Ed Deming is an internationally respected expert in statistical studies. He's the man who in 1950 convinced the Japanese that quality increases profits and that cheaper is by no means better. He advocates the proposition that the higher the quality in a product or service, the *less* it will cost. Why?

> A cheaply made product demands virtually the same raw materials, machinery, labor, and handling as its higher-quality brother. But many cheaply made items can't pass even the most cursory inspection, and a large number that do get to consumers fail early in actual use.

For any mail order entrepreneur, the first powerful lesson to be learned from the new surge toward quality is this: Buying from the lowest bidder can be very expensive indeed. Unless the offer is identical *in every way except price*, watch out for shortcuts that can damage what you are trying to accomplish in your business.

Second, do you really want to build your mail order business on a foundation of peddling junk? True, you *can* sell cheap products and services in large volume in the short term, but the ultimate consequences of product failure—and the inability of services to do what they are meant to do—can prove to be the undoing of a new enterprise.

When junk closely *resembles* better merchandise, a mail order operator who wants to handle better goods faces the challenge of getting that quality message across to consumers. The how-to's of doing that are covered in Chapter 6.

Next, consider some interesting ways of getting great mail order products outside of the ordinary channels.

TECHNIQUES FOR GETTING FABULOUS BUYS
ON CLOSE-OUTS

Rob Perlis devotes his business life to hunting down merchandise that is no longer wanted by manufacturers, jobbers and retailers, that is, clients who eventually realize that they have to take a loss on certain goods that are sitting in a warehouse accumulating costs. Turning these slow-moving items into at least *some* cash makes much more sense than continuing to store them in the hopes a regular customer will decide to buy it.

Some companies agree to do business with Perlis because his method of buying can help out a firm stuck with dead merchandise. Here's his policy:

- Rob will buy *anything* in *any quantity* as long as it's in good shape. If the packaging is damaged, he'll buy it anyway. There can be *no refusals to buy an item* that is represented as a close-out. Rob must take it, and all buys are final; there are no returns for *any* reason.

- All buys are cash on delivery.

Perlis is jokingly called a "scavenger" by some of his clients. One recent call from a retail chain provided four gross of huge inflatable bears. Just days later, Rob bought 20 calculators that figure calorie intake. Some finds are phenomenal even though the item's appeal had slowed to a crawl in normal distribution channels. Other items are so utterly useless that Rob himself tries to dump the lot instead of attempting to sell the products by mail order. It all works out because he buys at such steep discounts.

Since available quantities of close-outs can vary so widely, Rob sends out inexpensively printed bulletins to a small but valued list of buyers consisting of premium and incentive firms, retailers, and a handful of consumers. A catalog wouldn't work in this business since items can't be reordered once the close-out is gone.

This unusual operator *does* pass some savings on to his customers. It's the only way they would buy products that are still perfectly functional, but extremely tired in terms of salability.

Buying close-outs as Rob does takes cash and plenty of guts. It's a high-risk business that yields delightful surprises in merchandise, along with problem acquisitions. His biggest dilemma is that he can't select too far in advance what he'll be trying to sell next week.

We'll now look at another interesting possibility.

UNCOVERING RARE OPPORTUNITIES IN START-UP COMPANIES

Creative people who have the knack of dreaming up new products are often notoriously poor marketers. To some extent, the same thing is true of start-up firms and small- to medium-sized manufacturers. They usually have the ability to invent and build salable products, but sometimes lack the muscle or desire to market.

In many instances, the best possible news to a small manufacturer is that a mail order company is interested in exposing its products to thousands of targeted potential buyers. Hundreds of these managers would like nothing better than to give the burden of marketing to someone else, lock, stock, and barrel. Even when such a small product producer *is* actively involved in selling its wares through various means, it may still welcome the supplementary efforts of a mail order program.

Strangely, this is not a widely explored area for mail order entrepreneurs. Perhaps many of them shy away from the task of contacting companies in order to discover these opportunities. Whatever the case, it's a fruitful product source just waiting to be harvested.

Some of the cautions inherent in this area are the following:

- You must be able to get *finished products* from a company. Avoid at all costs a situation where the item is still in the idea stage and funding is needed to build them. Also, steer clear of cases where the would-be maker asks you to obtain orders *before* the products are made.

- In the case of a very new product entry, take a careful look at quality and performance. How much work has been done on proving the product? Remember, the maker may not have the same insights as you do regarding consumer acceptance.

- Make sure operating instructions are ready to go and are clear.

- While attractive packaging would be a nice bonus, it isn't really of primary importance since mail order buyers are more strongly oriented to the item than the carton. When they receive the package, the purchase has already been made.

Incredible breakthroughs are made when small manufacturers are systematically contacted by mail order companies. A simple letter can be sent to hundreds of firms asking them if they produce items suitable for mail order. A modified version of the letter shown earlier in this chapter can be used.

When *any* product is acquired from *any* kind of supplier, the following steps are critically important.

ASSURING A CONTINUING FLOW OF PRODUCTS AT STABLE PRICES

To any mail order customer, the ultimate aggravation is to comb through a catalog, meticulously select items, fill out the order form, write a check, and finally mail the envelope. Then, when expectations are at a high point several weeks later, a form letter arrives showing most of the selections out of stock or discontinued.

That happens to thousands of people every week. It is no wonder that many of them give up on a particular mail order source, or on buying by mail altogether. Failure to fulfil customer orders are suffered not only by small mail order firms but often by national merchandising giants. *Occasional* failures to fulfil orders are part and parcel of the mail order business, but frequent inability to deliver consumer orders reflects a problem in how products are screened during the selection process.

If your supplier can't commit to the continuing availability of a product for approximately six months from the time you place your initial order, you may run into difficulties. An exception would be a one-time promotion where you probably wouldn't be receiving additional orders months later. The six-month guideline is especially important if you are putting out a catalog that will be in buyer's hands for a long time.

It is not really reasonable to expect any manufacturer or distributor to commit beyond six months. Internal business considerations can bring about changes in a source's product lines and in the quantities produced. Importers are particularly hard put to control what will go on in distant lands and may not be able to assure supply beyond your current product needs.

When long-range commitments can't be made by your source of supply, the next best course of action is to find out what kind of quantities are presently in stock and how many are "on the water" (en route from overseas) or planned for production right *now*. You might be able to look at the answer and come up with a go/no-go decision.

Your *price* should also be "locked in" for at least six months. You can't be in a position where big jumps in the per item price are demanded on future orders. A supplier may hedge on this issue, explaining that external factors could cause increases. That's fair, given the uncertainty of world economies, raw material availability, and so forth. But you should still negotiate a reasonable ceiling on possible price boosts.

Style changes also have to be watched. You will almost certainly encounter consumer static if the red T-shirts they order are shipped in a vivid orange. At the same time, a $2 paperweight probably won't draw complaints if it's shaped a bit differently from the one pictured in your mailer.

For best results, get as much supplier assurance as possible that the specifications of your chosen products remain the same for the next months or so. Also, it's wise to use words like these in your mailer copy if you can't be absolutely sure about changes:

SIZE AND COLOR MAY VARY SLIGHTLY FROM ILLUS-TRATED ITEM

Here are tips on where to get lots of ideas on good mail order products.

WHERE TO GET VOLUMES OF PRODUCT INFORMATION AT LITTLE OR NO COST

Great clues on hot products and services are *everywhere*. Here's a rundown of the best resources:

Magazines That Carry Extensive Mail Order Advertising

Almost every consumer-oriented publication is loaded with mail order ads. When certain products are repeated from one edition to the next, you can bet they're doing business and are worthy of your attention.

Business Opportunity Magazines

Larger newsstands sell several good publications directed to the entrepreneurial market. You'll find product and service ideas in abundance, plus informative write-ups on new ventures.

Mail Order Promotions *You* Receive

Start a file of the offers you get in the mail. This is a valuable source of product and service ideas and hard-hitting mail order formats.

Retail Flyers

Virtually all weekend newspapers arrive with elaborate circulars promoting a wide range of items. Many of these goods are housewares, but you'll also discover ideas on gifts and other mail order categories.

Retail Stores

Spend some time going through local stores in your area. Gift stores, card shops, department stores, fashion boutiques, and even large hardware stores can generate ideas.

Catalogs

Obtain the catalogs put out by the six or eight leading retail/mail order giants. These companies make relatively few errors in selection, and they usually do a good job of presenting products and services in the best light.

Newspaper Ads

Scattered throughout the pages of your local daily are products and service mail order offers. Again, watch for *frequently repeated* ads since they probably indicate strong sales activity that warrants multiple runs.

TV Home Shopping Shows

Cable channels run many hours of mail order product programs. The operators of these shows are generally astute marketers who don't waste valuable air time on slow sellers. Product dialogue can provide terrific guidance on product copy.

Visit Importers, General Merchandise Distributors, And Other Suppliers

Nearly all suppliers maintain showrooms that enable you to review what's available. Try to pay special attention to the ones that stress wholesale only since they're the ones who specialize in supplying firms like yours.

Gift Shows

Major cities host several gift shows every year. They are usually held at a convention center over a period of several days. You should be able to gain entry at little or no cost. In these shows you'll find a vast array of suppliers, many of them eager to do business with you.

As you get into serious product scrutiny, this form should help you keep important information straight.

THE PRODUCT BUYING CHECKLIST

Change the form in Figure 3-2 as necessary to suit your operation, and make as many copies as you need to keep track of every product you review during your selection process.

Figure 3-2.

BUYING CHECKLIST

Supplier Information:
    Name of Company: _____

    Address: _____

    City: _____ State: _____ Zip: _____

    Telephone: (   ) _____

    Name of Contact: _____ Title: _____

    Date of Visit: _____

    Length of Time in Business: _____

    References:

    o _____

    o _____

    o _____

- -

Product Information:
    Describe Product: _____

    _____

    _____

    Colors Available: _____

    _____

    Describe Packaging: _____

    _____

    Box Dimensions: _____

    Shelf-Life Limitations: _____

    Sales Strength of Product According to Supplier: _____

    _____

    Future Availability: _____

    _____

    Anticipated Design Changes: _____

    _____

    _____

    Product Support Material Available:

    o   Photos   Yes _____   No _____

    o   Illustrations   Yes _____   No _____

    o   Copy   Yes _____   No _____

    o   Other: _____

Figure 3-2. Continued

Inspection of Product Sample (Rate 1 to 10):
o   Construction   _____
o   Uniformity   _____
o   Performance   _____
o   Estimated Durability _____
Other Products of Interest Offered by This Supplier: _____
_____
_____

- -

Shipping Information:
o   Amount of Freight from Source for Master Carton: $ _____
o   Master Carton Shipping Weight:_____
o   Individual Item Shipping Weight: _____
o   Describe Any Special Handling Required:_____
_____
o   Can Products Be Drop-Shipped?:   Yes _____ No _____
o   Supplier's Return Policy: _____
_____
o   Estimated Delivery Time:_____
o   Origin: _____
o   Delivery Method:_____

- -

Purchasing Information:
o   Target Quantity: _____   Required to Buy:_____
o   Target Cost: _____   Actual Cost:_____
o   Target Retail: _____   Actual Retail: _____
o   Payment Terms: _____
o   Price Increase or Reduction Anticipated? _____
_____
o   Quantity Discount Policy (Note Quantity Breaks):_____
_____
_____

- -

Figure 3-2. Continued.

Follow-up:

o   Additional Information to be Provided by Supplier: _____

_____

_____

o   To Be Provided by (Date): _____

o   Purchase Decision Promised to Supplier by: _____

_____

- -

Comments: _____

_____

_____

_____

_____

_____

_____

HOW TO PROSPER IN MEDIA ADVERTISING

In this form of mail order, ads are placed in print and/or broadcast media to trigger consumer response.

A well-designed ad offering an appealing product or service, run in the right medium at the correct time, has the elements needed to launch a torrent of sales, leads, or whatever other consumer action your ad requests. This chapter shows you how to build those success elements into a program of your own.

A LOOK AT THE STRENGTHS AND DRAWBACKS OF MEDIA ADVERTISING

Certain publications appeal to certain kinds of people. Virtually every national publication works hard and spends big money to reveal information like this about readers:

- Income range
- Occupations
- Age range
- Where readers live and, to the extent possible, *how* they live

And many more facts. These demographics provide strong clues about *what kind of features a particular audience wants to read,* and *what they are likely to buy,* and *how much they are apt to spend.* For example, one class of magazines can support mail order ads for costly numbered and signed lithographs. Another group of publications would better promote mail order sales of $19 a pair work shoes.

As a result of those extensive and continuing readership surveys, plus obvious visual evidence as to what types of mail order ads regularly appear in specific magazines, an advertiser can zero in pretty quickly on an apparently correct group of publications for a specific offer. A reasonable amount of research *will* reveal one or more promising categories of magazines, tabloids, newspapers, or other media.

If anything, there are really *too many* promising choices. When a mail order firm's budget is limited, which is usually the case, the only way to proceed intelligently is to *test* the likely media candidates. *Which* magazines of 20 possibilities are truly the best ones for your ad? Which daily newspapers of 5 in a region will produce a solid return on investment?

If broadcast is a tempting option, is a cable channel the way to go? Or are off-hour spots on a network the best choices? And how about the selling strength of drive-time radio?

Your primary challenge in media advertising is to *make the right choices*. This form of mail order is easier to execute than direct mail since you can initially do away with printing, mailing list acquisition, postage costs, and many other steps typically associated with sending promotions to consumers. But you will also discover that you have far less control over who and how many will see your ad in the particular issues you decide to run in. Even with the comforting readership statistics guiding your decisions, there are no ironclad guarantees about the performance of the issues you finally select.

Yet the potential payoff is well worth seeking. Media advertising pros know that careful investigation, wise product selection, and solid testing can lead rapidly to hefty profits. For newcomers to media advertising, modest local ads can parlay into national ad campaigns that generate huge sales. There *are* risks, but plenty of riches, too.

One aspect of media advertising that is considered the most lucrative by many experts is this: Orders received from readers become mailing lists of enormous value. Best of all, that growing population of established buyers is the *exclusive* property of the advertiser. So good media ads lay a foundation for highly effective *direct mail* promotions.

A leading media ad specialist now offers some invaluable guidelines for success in this fascinating aspect of mail order.

BASIC GUIDELINES FOR SELECTING THE HARDEST-HITTING AD MEDIUM

When certain measures are taken in the investigation of media, an intelligent choice is likely to result. *All* the items listed here should be checked:

Which Medium Reaches the Largest Number of *Qualified* Buyers?

Look at the total circulation numbers a medium reaches in both national and regional editions. Most newspapers, of course, will be regional only. Television and radio can also provide approximate audience numbers for various time slots.

The phrase *qualified readers* or viewers is a vital aspect here. You *must* have some evidence that a particular medium carries the kind of mail order advertising you want to do and that those who now advertise in the medium benefit to some degree. What good is a magazine that goes to 18 million grade school students if you're selling cigar cutters?

First, visit newsstands and begin collecting samples of the publications that look right to you. And list the radio stations and TV channels, if applicable. Then request media kits from each one, plus any other data they have available for potential advertisers.

This point bears repeating: If the literature sent to you *stresses* the availability of mail order space, and the medium itself contains lots of small ads selling products and services somewhat like yours, you can consider the audience qualified.

Don't forget *trade publications*. These are magazines, periodicals, and sometimes newsletters created *especially* for consumers or businesses in a specific industry. If your offer can be targeted that finely, this is a very strong category.

Will Costs Be Manageable?

Before you get too excited about a heavily circulated medium that's loaded with mail order ads, check out the cost. In comparing magazine space rates, use *one particular ad size* for all of your comparisons. For example, you might select a one-third page horizontal as a cost index, even if that may not be the ad size you finally decide to run.

Another part of making sure you compare apples to apples is to look *only* at the rate for a one-time ad, even though you'll probably buy multiple issues to receive a discount when decision time arrives.

Typically, the rate information mailed to you will look something like the schedule in Figure 4-1.

BLACK AND WHITE ADVERTISING RATES				
	1x	3x	6x	12x
1 page	$8,400	$8,000	$7,550	$7,150
2/3 page	6,500	6,175	5,850	5,500
1/2 page	5,125	4,850	4,600	4,350
1/3 page	3,600	3,400	3,250	3,050
1/6 page	1,900	1,805	1,700	1,600
1/12 page	1,000	950	900	850

Figure 4-1

In the example, the publication provides per ad price breaks up to a 12-issue commitment. During this rate comparison stage, disregard discounts offered by the various media, such as 2 percent off for cash, and so forth, since that would only complicate matters. These extra money-savers will be scrutinized more carefully later.

A simple break-even formula is all it takes to get a bearing on whether or not a given medium is within your range:

If your ad will cost $900 for one run and production (plus other expenses) comes to another $190, you have a total of about $1,090.

If your product sells for $25, and your markup gives you a $15-per-item profit margin, you'll have to sell 73 units to break even.

This exercise is rather frustrating during the formation of a mail order business since you won't really know *how* many products you'll sell prior to testing. At this point, it's *strictly* an estimate.

The $1,090 outlay is scary to almost any new mail order advertiser. It's all the more formidable if you get into a situation where you have to sell, say, 400 or 600 products through a single one-third page ad to break even! A number like 73 units really looks comfortable, especially when you consider that your later ads should do better than the very first one.

Does the Geographical Reach Make Sense?

You may be in a position where you want to confine sales to an area like the Midwest, the 11 western states, or some other defined region. If a medium doesn't deliver what you need, you might as well disqualify it.

Most media give you the option of selecting regional editions. These cost far less than national editions and might hit your target more efficiently.

Figure 4-2 is an example of a typical north American circulation map, provided with the rate information you'll receive.

Will the Medium Show Your Product or Service to Maximum Advantage?

Will an exquisitely detailed star sapphire look like anything in ordinary daily newspaper reproduction? Or does it demand color and the finer printing used in a quality magazine? Can a comparatively complex service story be told adequately in a half-page ad, or does it require a 30- or 60-second verbal description supported by a step-by-step demonstration via television?

No matter how great a deal you uncover in your search for a medium, it won't count for much unless it promises to be a suitable "billboard" for your offer.

Before we move on to a more detailed discussion about magazines as a powerful mail order medium, we'll look briefly at the standard method of equating costs for all media.

USING "COST PER THOUSAND" AS A CONVENIENT MEASUREMENT

When you finally have a file bulging with circulation numbers, ad costs, and other vital data, you'll want a simple method for comparing one medium with another. Cost per thousand is that method. It's used by media and ad agency people, so you'll find it useful to understand how it works. Cost per thousand neatly solves a problem like this:

Total North American Circulation: 429,948

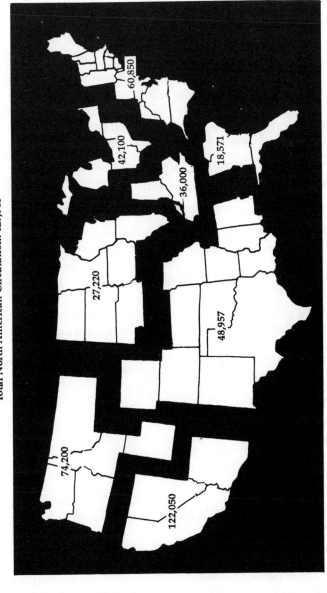

Figure 4-2. Example of a Magazine Circulation Map

One publication promises to give you 40,000 readers through an
$800 ad.

Another claims to deliver 200,000 potential buyers for a $3,000 ad.

One can be driven to the edge of madness trying to juggle the cost
versus audience size. The way to avoid that complexity is simply by
figuring out how much it will cost to reach 1,000 people. For example,
in the first case, the $800 ad that will be seen by 40,000 souls comes
out to about $20 per thousand, not including ad production costs. The
200,000 readers will cost a lot more to reach in terms of total outlay,
but the cost per thousand *is only $15*. A better deal if:

- You can budget the bigger cash expenditure.

- The audience is well qualified.

- Your audience is located where you want them to be.

Radio and TV rates can be equated the same way, but remember
to figure cost per thousand for *each time your message airs*.

THE POWER OF MAGAZINE ADVERTISING

Magazines clearly represent the mainstream of mail order media
advertising. Scarcely a product or service exists that has not been sold
through ads in magazines at one time or another. At last count, there
were well over 400 magazines with substantial distribution targeted
to the consuming public. They cover:

- Editorial

- Entertainment

- Fashion

- Home

- News

- Special interests

- Sports

- Youth

A list of today's hottest mail order publications would actually
be misleading since the darlings of the moment will in time give way
to a fresh group of powerful mail order magazines. Then, yet new

front runners will emerge. Present leaders in direct response are called *pilot publications*.

Big mail order spenders enjoy tremendous advantages by virtue of their ability to select position in the magazines they choose to carry ads. The following ad locations have been proven to get the best sales results:

- When an ad is placed toward the *front* of a magazine, it will tend to perform better. The first ten pages are prime territory.

- As you might expect, when an ad is easy for the reader to see, it sells more. That means it should contrast with adjoining material. For example, if your offer shows a bold headline and illustration, it will pop out if it's positioned with columns of straight text.

- *Right-hand pages* are generally more desirable, regardless of whether they're up front or toward the back of the magazine.

Small ads will not entitle an advertiser to special positioning. Only full-page or double-page spread buyers can successfully negotiate favorable ad location. In addition, most magazines will avoid inserting *any* small ads in the front of their publication. Typically, the back of the magazine is where the smaller ads are found in high density.

An *insert card*, similar to the one illustrated in Figure 4-3, is an expensive and effective mail order selling device. Several of these are bound into almost any magazine you pick up. Big advertisers buy a full page *plus* the preprinted insert, which is almost always in the form of a postage-paid business reply card. You've undoubtedly noticed that magazines will flop open to pages where the inserts are. That "bookmarker" phenomenon neatly assures both position and visibility.

Color sells better and can be a justifiable extra expense when a product lends itself to that approach. A gray plastic electronic device would be a questionable choice to run in color, but an imported tapestry demands it. Color can easily add 40 percent or more to your costs compared to a black and white ad of the same size. Also, you'll be compelled to buy larger space than you may need if you run color. For smaller ads, you may be able to request one color plus black or

Figure 4-3. Bound-in Insert Card

perhaps a background tint that increases visibility. Check the policy of each individual magazine to find out what your color options are.

Figure 4-4 provides a picture of a typical mail order response pattern in a monthly magazine.

Thus, for a monthly, about half the orders you'll receive will arrive in six weeks or so. The balance of your business will take several more months to come in. Magazines in the home category tend to sit on consumer coffee tables somewhat longer and, hence, have longer response times. Correspondingly, weekly magazines yield whatever results they're going to get in a shorter period of weeks.

Card decks are essentially postcard-size promotions that many magazine publishers send out to subscribers one or more times a year. Since card decks are sent *directly* to business-oriented readers, and are not delivered with the magazine itself, this interesting area is more appropriately discussed in Chapter 5, *Making Big Money by Mailing Direct to Buyers*.

Bingo cards, formally called reader service cards, are known to virtually every magazine advertiser. A postcard similar to the one in Figure 4-5 is bound into the back of most business-oriented publications.

Here's how Bingo cards work. Ads in the magazine carry lines that read

Circle #110 on Reader Service Card

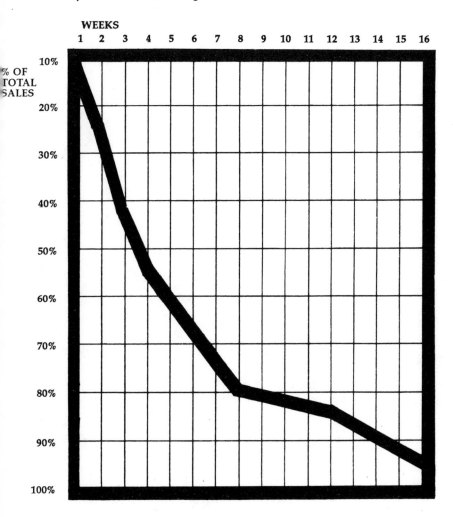

Figure 4-4. Monthly Magazine Response Curve

When a reader sees ads worthy of response, he or she circles the appropriate numbers on the Bingo card and then mails the card to the magazine. The reverse side of the card is set up in a business reply format, first class postage paid so it costs the inquirer nothing to mail.

When the card is received by the magazine, circled numbers are noted, and the inquirer's name and address information are for-

[ ] Please contact me with more information about the products/services advertised with these Reader Service Numbers.

100	101	102	103	104	105	106	107	108	109
110	111	112	113	114	115	116	117	118	119
120	121	122	123	124	125	126	127	128	129
130	131	132	133	134	135	136	137	138	139
140	141	142	143	144	145	146	147	148	149
150	151	152	153	154	155	156	157	158	159
160	161	162	163	164	165	166	167	168	169
170	171	172	173	174	175	176	177	178	179
180	181	182	183	184	185	186	187	188	189
190	191	192	193	194	195	196	197	198	199
200	201	202	203	204	205	206	207	208	209
210	211	212	213	214	215	216	217	218	219
220	221	222	223	224	225	226	227	228	229
230	231	232	233	234	235	236	237	238	239
240	241	242	243	244	245	246	247	248	249
250	251	252	253	254	255	256	257	258	259
260	261	262	263	264	265	266	267	268	269
270	271	272	273	274	275	276	277	278	279
280	281	282	283	284	285	286	287	288	289
290	291	292	293	294	295	296	297	298	299

Name _____

Title _____

Firm _____

Address _____

City _____

State _____ Zip _____

Phone (___) _____

Signature _____

[ ] Please enter my paid subscription to *TeleProfessional*... $29 for 6 bimonthly issues.

[ ] Payment enclosed. [ ] Please bill me.
[ ] Please charge my

_____ MasterCard _____ VISA account.

Card No. _____

Exp. Date _____ Bank No. (MC only) _____

Signature _____

Business Type (check one)
☐ Telecommunications/Telemarketing
☐ Insurance
☐ Financial Services
☐ Computer Services
☐ Hotel/Resort/Airlines Cust. Svc.
☐ Sales/Telemarketing Training
☐ Sales/Telemarketing Consulting
☐ Agency (Adv., Dir. Mktg., Mktg. Res.)
☐ Manufacturing
☐ Wholesale Distribution
☐ Retail/Catalog
☐ Other

Sales Volume (check one)
☐ Less than $1 Million
☐ $1-5 Million
☐ $6-10 Million
☐ $11-50 Million
☐ $50+ Million

Employee Size (check one)
☐ Less than 25
☐ 26-50
☐ 51-250
☐ 251-1,000
☐ 1,001+

Figure 4-5. A Reader Service ("Bingo") Card

54

warded to the appropriate advertisers. The advertiser then sends out whatever information was promised in its ad.

Many magazines work hard on turning these inquiries around efficiently, but it is not uncommon for an inquirer to wait weeks for a response from an advertiser. At least some of the blame for slow turnaround time must go to some advertisers who often do not take Bingo card leads as seriously as they should. One has to wonder why they bother to advertise.

One strong advantage to reader service cards is this: A magazine ad can be run *without* the space-eating reply section that's supposed to be filled out by the inquirer. A high percentage of ads in business-oriented magazines carry just an 800 toll-free telephone number and the reader service number, so available selling space can be maximized.

Remember: Ads with reader service numbers are used to attract inquiries, *not* direct sales.

Next is a review of newspapers as a mail order vehicle.

NEWSPAPERS SELL A FORTUNE IN PRODUCTS AND SERVICES

For reaching big numbers of consumers economically, no advertising medium beats newspapers. An enormous number of mail order operators spend a lion's share of their budgets on newspaper advertising. This despite some erosion in newspaper readership over past years due to increases in the quantity and quality of TV news coverage.

To provide a revealing look at the various mail order possibilities offered by major metropolitan newspapers, one paper in particular is profiled for you now:

In a U.S. city of about 1.5 million population, the afternoon paper reaches a total paid circulation of 432,425 for the daily edition and 509,688 for the Sunday paper.

In addition to choosing space in standard daily sections such as *general news, sports,* and *business,* advertisers can select these special sections:

Sunday	TV Section
	Color Magazine
	Travel
	Color Comics
	Book Review
	Arts & Entertainment
	Home/Real Estate
Monday	Fashion
	Business
Tuesday	Travel
	Business
Wednesday	Food
	Fashion
Thursday	Travel
Friday	Around Town
Saturday	Religion
	Weekend

This newspaper also offers a *special sections calendar* that points out expanded coverage planned on certain future dates. Two months are sampled here:

January	Hawaii
	Boat Show
	Super Bowl Preview
February	Easy Cooking
	Home Show

Thus, a newspaper mail order offer can effectively target a female, male, or mixed audience and to some extent can reach selected age categories. For example:

- Color Comics reach a slightly younger, more highly educated group (surprising as that may seem).

- Fashion, Easy Cooking, and other food sections would be more widely followed by women.

- Boats and various sports-oriented sections might be expected to attract more male readers.

Yet other choices have to be made by mail order advertisers. The following options are generally available:

ROP (run of paper) is simply anything printed in the regular pages of the newspaper. This is most often the choice when small ads are run. Small ROP ads have to be black and white.

Preprints are, as the name suggests, printed in advance and then inserted by the newspaper. This is costly, high-impact advertising used by the heavy hitters in mail order, such as record and book clubs.

Preprints can be inserted in the newspaper on a full cover age basis or for selected zip codes. The Sunday flat rate for full coverage in the paper we're discussing costs $20,400 for a four-page preprint—and that does *not* cover printing expenses.

So for start-up mail order companies on a tight budget, the answer is to run ROP ads in a section that will most likely be seen by the desired reader. Some newspapers offer zone editions that let the advertiser choose one or more parts (north, south, east, or west) of a metropolitan area and pay only for that coverage. Be sure to ask your paper if that kind of flexibility is available. It makes sense to use zone coverage when doing ad effectiveness testing, as you will see later.

Positioning of ads in newspapers is not as critical as it is in magazines, but up-front and right-hand pages still do marginally better. Gutters (center) positions don't usually do as well. Generally, bigger ads pull better, but debate still rages as to whether a full-page will do twice as well as a half-page. The *cost per response* remains the critical factor. Again, testing will eventually tell the story.

Mail order advertisers must find out how many rate schedules a newspaper uses and be assured that they are quoted the best available rates. As a case in point, the paper in our example has both a retail and a general rate. For a one-column by 8-inch ad on a 26-week contract (24 weekly insertions during a 26-week period), the rates compare this way:

Retail rate $34.44 per ad for full coverage

General rate $66.85 per ad for full coverage

That's a *huge* difference. Mail order firms almost always qualify for the lower retail rate since the consumer is given a definite number to call or place to go to make the purchase.

Before we move on to television and radio, here is a word about classified advertising.

USING LOW-COST CLASSIFIED ADS TO BUILD A VALUABLE MAILING LIST

Comparatively cheap classified ads are used to enormous advantage by successful mail order firms. An ad costing a few dollars can bring in the names of hundreds of prospects for whatever you are selling. A typical example is illustrated in Figure 4-6.

Figure 4-6. A Low-Cost Classified Ad Strictly for List-Building

WILDLIFE EXPEDITIONS

For free brochure, write
(address)

By simply offering a free catalog or "more information," a mailing list can swell from a few hundred to many thousands of active buyers. A majority of these people are interested specifically in the area emphasized in your small classified ad, so they are *qualified prospects* for the most part.

In the best list-building classified ads, no attempt whatever is made to sell a product or service. The *only* inducement that works is more information.

Some companies are successful in charging a nominal amount for their catalog. An example is the ad pictured in Figure 4-7.

Figure 4-7. A Classified Ad Designed to Cover Your Cost For Catalog Distribution

FINE SILK TREES AND FLOWERS

Hundreds of elegant hand-made, lifelike
arrangements. FREE full-color catalog only
$3. Refunded on first purchase.

(Address)

This exceptionally potent method for using newspapers to identify hot buyers can and *should* be used in addition to any other mail order approaches underway. By virtue of its nominal cost, it doesn't require much budget juggling.

To make classified ads work for you, use *only* those newspapers that carry heavy help-wanted Sunday classified sections. That's where you'll find lots of ads for various product and service sales. Neighborhood "throw-away" papers or local shoppers aren't much good for the purpose of list building. You need a classified section that is routinely scanned by job seekers, bargain hunters, and the curious.

It is important to note that magazines, while more costly, can also work extremely well for list building ads like the ones just reproduced.

YOUR INTRIGUING POSSIBILITIES IN TV AND RADIO

Cable television brings the selling power of television into the reach of almost every mail order operator. Rates are reasonable, and coverage is excellent in most cases. In most viewing areas, an advertiser has a choice of channels, each offering very definite viewer characteristics. For example:

- A product or service of special appeal to women can be run on *Lifetime Television* where programming is strongly slanted to female audiences. In Lifetime's 4 P.M. to 12 A.M. time slot, a 30-second commercial costs $90 and reaches some 610,000 cable households in a three-county Seattle area. Morning rates are lower still.

- Product or service offers directed to a male market can be aired on widely viewed ESPN, the total sports network. Here, a 30-second commercial costs $190 in the same 4 P.M. to 12 A.M. time slot, reaching the same 610,000 households just described.

Cable executives claim that their audiences are more upscale than people in noncable households and watch more television. They also say that cable provides the visual impact no other non-television medium can deliver. The latter point can't be disputed.

Commercial televison is generally much more costly, but it should still be checked out since local network affiliates might have bargains available for advertisers from time to time.

Production expenses for a 30-second commercial don't necessarily *have to* run into astronomical figures, but home-made and tight budget spots *do* almost always look that way. Also, the cable channel will want certain quality standards to be met. Therefore, an advertiser has to make a serious commitment to televison advertising by means of (1) a nicely executed piece of video and (2) purchase of enough 30-second spots to get the point across.

In today's economy, a 30-second commercial of the most modest proportions can run as low as $2,500 to produce. That includes a simple product or service demonstration with a few striking visuals, professional scripting and narration, and studio-quality video.

For testing in a local market, figure two spots per day over a two-week period. At $130 per commercial, that's $1,820 for the air time. So a solid cable televison test should total about $4,500.

Radio can work well for mail order. One auto parts entrepreneur developed a device that replaces the standard cap on a tire valve. It visually indicates a low tire, thus saving a driver the task of manually removing each cap and checking the tire pressure in the traditional way. A set of four retails for about $12, a price that could attract impulse, call-in purchases.

Such an item certainly *could* be dramatically depicted in a televison spot. But the concept in this case is simple enough to be clearly described by voice alone, and creation of a radio commercial is far less costly than a televison spot; the test totaled just over $2,000, a bit less than half the cost of cable television.

Station format largely determines what kind of people you'll reach in terms of age, income level and, to some extent, gender.

The choices are

• Heavy rock	• Talk
• Top 40	• Country
• Ethnic	• News
• Oldies	• Easy listening
• Pop	• Standards
• Classical	

Rock will get to a mixed audience 18 to 24 years of age. Classical stations are preferred primarily by affluent adults age 35 and older.

Some formats are not quite as easy to peg, and interviews of key station managers will help you toward a better understanding of who the audience really is.

One factor to consider is this: Since morning and afternoon drive times are peak listener periods for radio, can consumers sitting in traffic be expected to call in on impulse after your commercial? Another caution is; Since radio is so fragmented (relatively small groups of people follow certain kinds of formats), can you reach your total market through just one station or do you need several?

Selecting the right advertising medium or combination of media is one of the big challenges in mail order. *Testing* is the only way to come up with the best solutions.

IDENTIFYING THE RIGHT MEDIA FOR YOUR MAIL ORDER PROGRAM

When money is tight, the right mail order advertising choices have to be made as rapidly as possible. You must do everything you possibly can to decide if you're going to use magazines, direct mail, newspapers, TV or radio—or some combination thereof. Unfortunately, there are *no* set recipes for buying mail order media. In fact, two different advertisers offering a similar product may end up using two entirely divergent approaches, and both can nicely meet their sales objectives.

Testing is the most important process in putting together a money-making mail order program. Sophisticated merchants are almost always amused when they hear someone say, "That's a great ad" or "What a clever commercial." It may very well be beautiful or entertaining, but the *only* measure that means anything is; Does it *sell* effectively? Quite often, downright ugly or awkward ads outproduce the pretty ones!

Ideally, a new mail order offer might be exposed on a test basis in a couple of strong magazines, in a newspaper, in broadcast commercials, and via direct mail. More realistically, budget constraints allow much less latitude than that. But whatever the media choice for a test happens to be, the underlying objective is this:

Get the *lowest cost per response* so the fewest number of sales
are needed to break even

One very successful mail order gift firm tests two magazines and two
or three cable TV channels in addition to doing regular mailings to
old customers. That approach rarely fails. The steps taken by this
company are now described.

TESTING TO PROVE MEDIA EFFECTIVENESS

Definite testing goals have to be decided on before *any* money is spent
on a particular advertising medium. The mail order gift firm is after
the following information:

Which Magazine and TV Channels Will Produce the Desired Results for the Item to be Promoted?

The *same* ad is run in two magazines and on two or three TV channels.
It's important in such a test to *key the ad* so responses can be accurately attributed to the correct medium. For example, call-in responses
from one magazine could arrive on one inbound telephone line and
responses from the other publication on a different line. Or buyers
might be instructed in different ads to ask for different department
numbers. In the case of mail-in coupons, the design or typestyle on
the coupon holds the key to its source.

Many magazines can handle split runs for buyers of large ads.
Half the book's circulation carries one ad, and the other half a different
ad. This will show the stronger ad *only* if the split can be done in the
same geographical area (if half the readers are in the south and the
other half resides in the great plains, a split is of no use since regional
buying preferences enter the picture and skew the results).

If a split is not available to you as a small advertiser, run different ads
in two *similar* magazines one month; then reverse them the next month.

How Small Can the Ad Be?

Answer: As small as it can possibly be, but still tell the story and
be seen easily by consumers. Generally, ads intended to attract inquiries can be smaller than ads selling products or services.

Here are just a few of the options available to you in testing product or service ads:

- One large ad in one publication can be tested against two smaller ads in another, similar, magazine during the same month.

- One large ad in one publication can be tested against two or more smaller ads in a similar magazine run over a period of two months or more.

- A test can be conducted to determine whether a half-page ad does twice the business of a quarter-page ad. If the quarter-page ad holds its own, how exactly does the cost per response stack up to the larger ad? And does it make sense to find out how an even smaller ad would do?

What *Kind* Of Ad and Commercial Will Generate the Strongest Response?

At least two concepts are tested to find the answer.

Here are the elements that are most often subject to alternative approaches:

- Headline
- Layout
- Offer

It isn't unusual for the gift company to come up with two distinctly different ads that both promise to hit hard. So both warrant testing. Price differences can also be tested. In one instance, the gift firm ran an ad quoting a retail price of $9.49 for an ornate picture frame. It ran the same ad in a different magazine, but quoted $9.99 for the frame. The higher price did better. By all evidence, people tended to ignore the cents in that price.

Remember, in testing *control* is vital. Tracking the numbers and accurately attributing the sources of sales has to be done meticulously.

By asking the right questions, big money can often be saved in buying media.

MONEY-SAVING TIPS ON BUYING MEDIA

You can save significant money by being aware of various breaks that are sometimes available to advertisers. Areas to explore are the following:

Vendor Programs (Co-op Advertising)

If you decide to promote products made by major manufacturers, those sources may agree to pay all or a portion of your media advertising costs. For example;

> An aggressive china and crystal seller in a western U.S. city asks its three key sources to chip in on full-color monthly mailers. The manufacturers each get one-third of the ad space for their products, and their names are prominently displayed. Willard Grabert, marketing manager of the mail order firm, says sales are increasing 60 percent per quarter in this program.

In addition to direct mail, Sunday newspaper magazine section color ads are run. Still, promotional expenses for the mail order firm are tiny. *Everybody* benefits. If you buy products or services from a well-known national firm, it *definitely* pays to ask them if they'll support a co-op advertising program.

Remnant Space

Every advertising medium has leftover space or time on their hands now and then. They would much rather *sell* this remnant space at extremely low rates than fill it with editorial material that doesn't bring in any cash.

Such space tends to pop up close to deadlines, so it won't help to inquire about it weeks in advance. If you have a small ad or a 60-second commercial ready, a call just before publication or air time might pay off.

Special Print Media Price Breaks

- Frequency Discounts: Virtually all media offer frequency discounts. The more times you agree to run your ad, the less each one will cost. Thus, in a testing program, your per insertion cost will invariably run more since you probably should not commit to an extensive campaign. But when a medium is a proven winner, steep per ad cost breaks can be had by signing a contract for many runs.

- Per Inquiry Arrangements: In some instances, an advertiser can successfully negotiate a deal whereby each inquiry costs a certain amount, but there is very little or no charge for the space itself. To track the inquiry count in such a program, the medium will receive the orders or inquiries and then sell them to the advertiser.

- Seasonal Discounts: During slow-selling months, some media will cut normal rates. The problem is, of course, that these off periods will not likely produce good sales results. Still, if your cost per inquiry looks good because of lower media costs, a slow season test at discounted rates might work out okay for you.

- Barter: Trading your merchandise or services for ad space is rare today, but may still be available at times, especially with small publications. Again, it doesn't hurt to ask.

- Mail Order Space: Don't forget to ask if special mail order rates are available. These prices are considerably lower than general rates. Mail order rates usually apply to space in the back of a publication, among numerous other mail order ads. Regardless of the crowd, small mail order operators often do well in these special sections.

One final word about media advertising. It pertains to methods of buyer response.

USING FAX, TOLL-FREE TELEPHONE AND MAIL TO BUILD BUYER RESPONSE

To determine the response methods used by a sampling of mail order advertisers, a random group of 60 were selected from the pages of a leading national magazine. Here are the results:

Twenty-seven provide an address and toll-free 800 telephone number.

Five show an address, an 800 number, and their local phone number.

Two print just an 800 number (both are sizable firms with large full-color ads).

Fifteen publish their address and local telephone numbers.

One gives only a local phone number.

Seven provide only their address.

One supplies an address, local phone number, and a fax number.

One displays address, 800 number, and fax.

One shows address, local phone, 800 line, and fax.

So the most widely used combination is clearly a mailing address and an 800 toll-free phone number, with address and local phone running a strong second.

A total of 36 advertisers use 800 lines for taking inquiries, making the inbound toll-free call a staple in this business.

It is rather surprising that fax capability is present in just 3 of 60 mail order ads. That number has to increase dramatically over the years.

Other interesting items are the exclusive use of *only* an address in seven ads and the utilization of a local phone alone in one ad.

Obviously, a toll-free number makes response easy for consumers, and that's a key factor in getting maximum response.

It should be noted that the 60 ads surveyed presented products and services ranging from information about South American expeditions to the direct sale of California almonds. Some ads were for selling, others for attracting inquiries by means of offering catalogs or other kinds of additional information.

According to this informal look at response methods, a small mail order company *can* function adequately with a mailing address and local phone number; consumers who are interested enough *will write* in order to inquire or purchase. *But an 800 number does certainly boost the number of responses*. And fax should be part of future plans, since machines will be less expensive and thus more widely used.

To many, direct mail represents the promised land in the mail order industry. The next chapter is devoted to that intriguing approach to making money.

CHAPTER 5

MAKING BIG MONEY BY MAILING DIRECTLY TO BUYERS

Promotions mailed or delivered directly to consumers or businesses give you the extraordinary ability to select your markets precisely and to impart exactly the kind of messages you want to send to those prospective buyers. Direct mail also eliminates the severe space limitations imposed by high ad and broadcast rates. Catalogs offering scores or even hundreds of items can be put into the hands of your buyers at acceptable cost.

In addition, mailings cut through the narrow reach of TV signals and print circulation. National and worldwide markets become available to you. You are limited only by the power of your mailing list.

This chapter is devoted to exciting and high-impact direct mail.

CONSUMER DIRECT MAIL PROGRAMS

People buy by mail for an array of reasons, but these are the primary ones:

- Convenience and elimination of travel expense
- Avoidance of high-pressure selling
- Discovery of unique products
- Wider selection

- A perception that savings will be realized, although that is almost never the case

To give you an idea of the enormous size of the U.S. consumer market, consider these figures pertaining to the age group a generation older than baby boomers:

There are more than 60 million shoppers over age 50 in the United States. They control 50 percent of this nation's discretionary income and 77 percent of all United States assets. *They spend $800 billion annually, and 85 percent of them regularly buy through the mail!*

How do you reach them? They can be precisely targeted by direct mail. Mailing lists available through brokers let you select exact ages, neighborhoods, occupations, and other key prospect features.

Due to that ability to target highly specific markets, a mail order operator can create a promotional package that speaks the prospect's language in no uncertain terms.

With 60 million of these over-50 spenders all over the United States, *plus* some 76 million baby boomers, a direct mail operator *has no choice* but to do some very careful selecting. If there is one stumbling block in kicking off a consumer direct mail program, it is figuring out just where to begin. If you can budget funds for a mailing to 20,000 prospects, where *is* that target group when the biggest-spending population of potential buyers is 136 million?

Most entrepreneurs who face that dilemma select a group close to home for starters. This makes the servicing of accounts far easier. Then, as the business grows, mailings can be sent to more distant addresses.

In consumer direct mail, an approach like the following can work well:

Start a direct mail program by choosing the strongest possible prospect characteristics for your products or services. Then try to find a list that gives you *exactly* what you want.

At the same time, allocate enough money to run classified ads in carefully selected magazines, newspapers, or both. Offer free information so you can start building *your own* strong consumer prospect list.

The faster you can establish your own list and get away from renting mailing lists, the better off you'll be.

Remember, many of the consumers from your rented list will buy and/or inquire, thus becoming part of your private list. So your goal of becoming *list independent* can sometimes be reached quickly.

A highly respected advertising agency executive was asked what he believed were the three most important components in direct mail. He replied, "The list, the lists and the list." Because there is some weight in that analysis, a later chapter is given entirely to mailing lists.

Now a look at mailing to companies.

MAKE BIG MONEY MAILING TO BUSINESS FIRMS

Products and services purchased by companies are far more predictable than those bought by consumers. Businesses buy office supplies, educational programs and materials, furniture and accessories, and a multitude of other things that help them operate more efficiently or more stylishly.

One clear advantage in mailing to companies is this: The total population of prospective firms is easy to identify compared to consumers. A mail order operator on an extremely tight budget can even skip the renting of lists in favor of combing through the classified telephone directory in a do-it-yourself list-building process. This is often done successfully, but has some drawbacks. For example,

> A classified telephone book listing does not describe the size of a firm in terms of number of employees. And more often than not, it's difficult to be certain what *kind* of company you're looking at. In addition, you won't get the name of the buyer from a phone book display ad.

At the same time, a mail order operator can acquire business listings from a local chamber of commerce, from trade magazine ads, and from various other sources. Many of those directories *do* include information that helps you intelligently select prospects. More about various business-to-business prospect sources in Chapter 7 on list building.

As just mentioned, a *specific contact name* is very important in promoting direct to companies by mail. Ideally, you'd be able to include something like *James F. Scott, Plant Manager,* in your address. In a firm with many employees, your direct mail piece will receive scant attention if it isn't directed to a specific individual. In contrast, a consumer mailer to a household *will* in most cases be read by somebody who lives there, it is hoped a responsible adult.

Here's a business-to-business direct mail strategy that can do a good job of getting your promotion into the hands of qualified company buyers.

CARD DECKS

Many business-oriented magazines and trade publications send card decks to their subscribers one or more times each year. Both sides of an actual size card are shown in Figure 5-1.

Most of these promotional cards are used to generate *inquiries* by offering information or free catalogs to readers. But there are usually a few cards in each deck mailing that go for the close on books, posters, and various other small items. The advertiser's address usually appears on the mailing side of the card. Dewey Johnson, publisher of Co-Op Postcards in Minneapolis, provided these ratios:

> Response to an average card in a mailing is 1/4 percent to about 1 percent. When sent to a subscriber list of 50,000, 1/2 percent translates to 250 inquiries. Of these, about 90 percent will include a name and address. That amounts to $3.60 per inquiry.

One company selling wooden blinds ran a card offering a 12-page brochure. They got a 2.4 percent response, or 1,325 leads.

Typically, a card costs somewhere between $600 and $1,800, depending on the magazine's list size, which generally falls in a range between 20,000 and 100,000 or more companies. Prices are for camera-ready art; if you need the magazine's help in composing the ad and mailing side of the card, the cost goes up.

"Live" area (available advertising space) of each card is only 3 inches by 5 inches, and one-third of that has to be used for prospect response information such as name, address, phone number, and so forth. So your message must be exceedingly brief and to the point. A Chicago-based card expert provides these layout guidelines:

- Select the *two* strongest selling features for your card and drop the others. Keep the copy absolutely straightforward.

Figure 5-1. A Promotional Postcard

Front

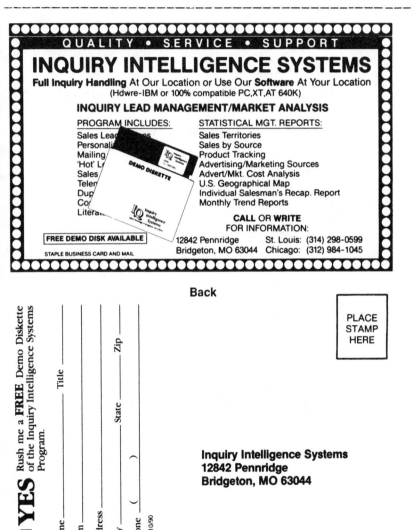

Back

- Run either a picture of your product or a long headline, but you probably won't have sufficient space for both.

- Photos will generally not do well in a card format since the reproduction size has to be so small. Line drawings do better.

- Select a *distinctive typeface* so your card contrasts with others in the deck.

- *Offer something.* Either sell a product or extend the prospect an opportunity to request more information.

- The mailing side of the card has to conform to the business reply specifications set forth by the U.S. Postal Service.

If you plan on selling to other businesses, card decks should be checked out as a strong possibility, especially if you can identify a magazine that goes to your markets. If you sell by means of a two-step process (inquiry first, then close), cards make particularly good sense. How else can you reach about 20,000 prospects for $600 or so?

Whether your mail order business promotes to consumers, businesses, or both, the next section is vitally important.

THE BIGGEST, FASTEST PAYOFF: MAILING TO EXISTING CUSTOMERS

A mail order business has truly arrived when it has successfully built a large base of active buyers. Old customers are *much* more likely to respond to new promotions than are people who see your ad or mailer for the very first time.

Research has proven beyond any doubt that ads, mailers, and broadcast messages don't have much impact the first few times they reach people. That's why media tests don't really prove anything unless they provide repeated exposures. A new advertiser is an unknown quantity to consumers and business buyers.

But a prior buyer knows and trusts you. There is instant recognition of your company name, so sales resistance has been broken down permanently.

Wendy Song mails a catalog of oriental specialty items. When she started in business four years ago, promotions were all in the form of small display ads in women's magazines. Wendy offered her catalog free of charge, so her sole objective was to *attract inquiries*.

At that stage in the development of her business, Wendy was spending almost every cent of advertising budget on building a list. By her third year of operation, only *10 percent* of that budget goes to obtaining new leads. A full 90 percent is spent strictly on *established buyers*. The woman's list numbers some 6,000 more or less active buyers, with 100 to 200 new customers added monthly. Wendy's definition of an active buyer is a consumer who has made any size purchase within the last four months.

Advertising for new inquiries can never be dropped entirely in *any* direct mail program. The best customer lists will eventually erode if new blood is not continually infused. People move or change their buying patterns, and gradual list shrinkage inevitably occurs.

Media ads can in some instances be effective in selling old customers or noncustomers who begin to recognize your ads. But it's cheaper by far to concentrate on selling those past buyers by direct mail.

Building a powerful base of active buyers is just one part of intelligently conducting a direct mail operation, as you'll discover now.

ZEROING IN ON SPECIFIC MARKETS

To start off on the right foot in direct mail, you must first have a crystal-clear picture of *who your best customers will be, and where they are*. Here are several examples of how some firms have cleared that hurdle:

- A company specializing in products for hunters and sports men and women buys lists of *known gun owners*. That audience is far more apt to purchase the gear offered in this company's catalog.

- Mail order buyers of food specialties are targeted by a firm selling gourmet kitchen utensils. On the flip side, a mail order seller of fine cookware buys lists of consumers who have recently purchased hard-to-find food items by mail.

- A company selling sales training programs to corporations mails exclusively to companies that have ten or more outside salespeople on their payroll.

Whether you mail to consumers or businesses, targeting of that kind is *essential*. Yet one of the most common errors committed by new mail order firms is to spend money on markets that are not ideally suited for the offered products or services. In the earliest planning stages of a direct mail campaign, these questions have to be considered:

IN MAILING TO CONSUMERS	IN MAILING TO COMPANIES
• Do they have a history of buying by mail?	• Is the firm engaged in a business that would be right for your offer?
• If so, have they purchased products or services similar to those you offer?	• If so, are they likely to buy by mail?
• If your offer is male or female oriented, will you be able to get your mailer to the correct person?	• Can you obtain a list that includes the name and title of the buyer?
• Are these people generally in an age group that should respond to what you are selling?	• Should your target firms employ a certain minimum number of employees so your efforts will be worthwhile?
• Are these prospects at an income level where they can afford what you are selling?	• Will you be able to identify *all* the departments in a firm that might order from you?

- Are your prospects geographically situated so you can service buyers?

- In addition to minimum company size guidelines, should you also establish *maximum* size guidelines?

By giving thought to those questions, you will successfully narrow the focus of your mailing program, thus hitting desired targets with far greater accuracy. Equally important, you'll be able to do some serious planning as to the *contents and tone* of your mailing; once you zero in on definite types of prospects, your sales message can be *more effectively customized for a defined market*. Some examples follow.

In both consumer or business mailings, direct mail packages generally resemble one of the three discussed next.

BASIC COMPONENTS OF EFFECTIVE DIRECT MAIL PACKAGES

There's an almost endless list of ways to design a direct mail package. But the three illustrated in Figures 5-2, 5-3, and 5-4 are the classic, time-proven formats.

Figure 5-2 is a mailing used to obtain *inquiries* and utilizes an envelope to hold its various components.

Figure 5-2. A Mailing Package for Generating Inquiries

Now we'll go into some detail about each component in the package.

Reply Card

The reply card is intended to capture a prospect's name, address, and telephone number plus identify the inquirer's main interest area so follow-up can be done in a multi-step selling process.

Effective lead-generating reply cards include a request for free information, similar to this:

YES! Please send me your free 24-page catalog

An inquiry-generating reply card should be printed on card stock, with the flip side in a business reply format, since no envelope is needed for a remittance,

Promotional Piece

The promotional piece provides a description of the products and services, usually combined with information about the firm's general capabilities. Since this mailer is part of a multi–step selling process, it may not get highly specific about products and often doesn't quote prices; the objective is to *heighten prospect interest* so recipients send in the card.

Cover Letter

A letter in the inquiry-generating direct mail package emphasizes these areas:

- The prospect's needs, and how your products or services will address those needs
- Your reliability as a product or service source
- Your expertise in the industry

Remember, when you have effectively targeted specific consumer or business markets, you should be in a position to talk about some of the *definite characteristics* of those markets. That is best done in the cover letter. For example, one paragraph might read.

Exceptionally quiet and compact conveyor systems are the features many plant managers demand in your industry. Our 700 series is designed for companies like yours.

Words like those are far more meaningful to a prospect than are generic statements.

The Mailing Envelope

The envelope holds all the components just listed. You can have a message printed on the left side of the envelope. In our example situation, it might read

> FINALLY . . . a conveyor system designed precisely for your needs!
> Details inside.

Figure 5-3 shows an envelope mailing used to obtain orders (*not* inquiries) for merchandise or services. It's different from the inquiry mailing because it has to accommodate a customer's order and payment. Thus, an order form and return envelope are of the utmost importance in this package.

**Figure 5-3. This Envelope Mailing Asks for the Order.
The Promotional Piece Includes the Order Form**

Here's a brief rundown on the components in this package:

Combined Promotional Piece/Order Form

This is simply a description of the products and/or services being sold. The basic elements are

- A photo or drawing

- Descriptive copy
- Ordering information, including prices

Such a piece can consist of a half-sheet showing just one product, all the way up to a catalog of many bound or separate pages.

Mailing Envelope

Reply Envelope

A promotional piece can double as the order form, as illustrated in Figure 5-3, or separate pieces can be used, as shown in Figure 5-4.

Figure 5-4. This Package Asks for the Order, and Provides a Separate Order Form

In Figure 5-4, a completely separate order form is enclosed in the package. There are two advantages here: (1) your customer still has possession of the promotional piece after making a purchase, and later purchases might result, and (2) if you change prices, only the order form has to be reprinted, *not* the promotional piece.

Self-mailers are considerably less costly to produce since all components are printed on one sheet of paper. Figure 5-5 illustrates a typical self-mailer that can be set up to obtain either leads *or* sales:

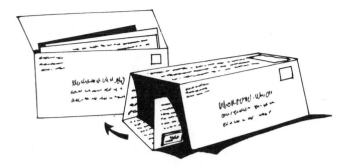

Figure 5-5. Format for a Self-Contained Piece. It Turns Into An Envelope for Return of an Order or Inquiry

Each vital component has to be included in a self-mailer. These are

- A mailing panel that carries the prospect's address and possibly some copy that builds prospect interest.

- Product or service pictures and descriptive copy.

- An order form that can be detached and mailed. *Or* an inquiry section if the piece is lead generating.

- When the self-mailer is intended to get orders, an envelope can be included. It tears off the piece at a perforation and can be folded and sealed so it's perfectly suitable for mailing.

- Even a cover letter can be printed in a well-planned self-mailer.

Generally speaking, self-mailers tend to *look* more like "junk mail" than envelope mailings, so may not always command the same respect from prospects.

We'll move on to catalog mailings, one of the most powerful selling tools in the direct mail industry.

CATALOG MAILINGS

A beginning mail order operator on a stringent budget has to carefully consider the following question:

If each catalog costs $1.25 or more to produce, and postage runs about $1.00, does it make good business sense to go ahead and mail this costly package to thousands of unproven prospects?

To many start-up mail order companies, the answer is no. Big, costly catalogs are mailed *only* to those who have already purchased or to parties who have specifically requested the book through a media ad or mailer designed to generate just such a lead.

Smaller catalogs of, say, 12-page length, *can* be sent almost as economically as one of the mailings described earlier. So it could be practical to send a smaller book out to thousands of prospects.

Figure 5-6 illustrates the components in a standard catalog mailing.

Figure 5-6. Typical Catalog Components Can Be Bound Into Large Books, or Enclosed as Separate Sheets in Smaller Books

Most catalogs work effectively with a number of order forms bound into the book. Pages in front include

- A cover letter
- Ordering information

If the book itself is expected to remain valid for six months or so before reprinting is necessary, prices may be included with product descriptions. This approach is also a must if the catalog is large, since customers would be annoyed at having to refer continually to a separate price list as they're going through the book. Smaller catalogs, and those subject to frequent change, *can* refer prospects to a separate order form/price list.

Envelopes for customer orders can be bound into the catalog or be enclosed separately.

In setting up a catalog, a carefully planned product numbering system is essential. This system has to identify clearly not only products but color choices, different sizes, and any other variations available to buyers. Bigger books should also carry a table of contents if several product categories are presented.

Catalogs continue to do a selling job over a much longer period of time than standard mailers. They are often retained by consumers and businesses for future reference. It is not unusual for a catalog mailing to get results up to a year or more after the mailing is sent.

Equally important, catalogs get a higher number of multiple-item sales than smaller promotions, so the average order is larger. This helps justify the higher production and mailing costs.

Effective follow-up to a catalog mailing can consist of

- Special sale announcements on items in the book
- Supplementary pages that introduce additions to certain product groups

These tactics keep your company name in the minds of prospects, and they *do* stir up later sales.

No doubt you've seen plenty of generic catalogs in your mail over the years. These are nicely printed books, large and small alike, turned out in huge quantities by manufacturers or distributors, and used by local mail order operators. A little white space is left on the front and back covers for imprint of the local company's name, address, and phone number.

You can buy as many catalogs as you need to cover your list and then have a printer insert your firm name in the appropriate white space. Per copy prices are usually lower for generic catalogs than you'd pay for a small quantity of home-made books by virtue of the enormous number printed; sometimes 1 million or more are turned out in one run.

Generic catalogs are frequently used by electronic consumer chains, large drugstore chains, office supply stores, auto parts dealers and similar big retail networks. Some gift and specialty merchandise distributors also put out these stock catalogs.

While generic catalogs may enable you to acquire a decent mailing piece at low cost, they really do *look* generic. Another big drawback is; This approach keeps you from developing your own unique "look" and merchandise selection since you are stuck with the items preprinted in the catalog pages.

In sharp contrast to the 150-year-old tradition of selling by catalog, here are a couple of comparatively recent direct mail innovations.

SELLING BY VIDEO AND AUDIOCASSETTE

A videotape can be reproduced and sent to prospects at about the same cost as a nicely printed mailer. This is done in business-to-business direct mail with great effectiveness because of these circumstances:

- Some products and services must be seen to be fully appreciated. A video can get complex and highly visual points across with tremendous drama.

- Many manufacturing facilities are impressive and *should* be shown off to prospects to help the sale along. A video can capture plant impressions as no photograph can.

- A vast majority of prospect firms have VCRs onsite, so there is rarely a problem in conveniently viewing a promotional video.

Sales presentations of about five minutes total running time are just about right for a package like this. A quality video costs about $1,000 per minute to produce, and copies are so cheap that the sender rarely seeks return of the tapes from prospects.

In consumer direct mail, cassette tapes are used more often than video. An audiotape up to 20-minutes in length can be produced professionally for less than $1,000, and copies go for under $1.00 each. A consumer *service* can be effectively presented via audiotape, but product sales obviously don't fit this voice-only medium.

Direct mail packages for both video and audio presentations should include cover letters *and* reply cards or order forms, as illustrated in Figure 5-7.

Figure 5-7. Mailing Components for a Video Presentation

We turn now to a money-saving direct mail method.

SLASHING COSTS THROUGH COOPERATIVE MAILINGS

Some new direct mail firms successfully hook up with ongoing companies on shared mailings. Christine DiForza sells a quality line of locally made cosmetics products, and she worked out this arrangement:

"I wanted to get my facial care product promotions to at least 30,000 women every four months, but the cost was way more than I could manage. While I was trying to solve those expense problems, I met a lady and her husband who were involved in selling a line of cookbooks to homemakers by direct mail. I proposed combined mailings and a shared cost deal with them. They agreed to try it.

"It costs me about 40 percent less to reach my market than it would if I was carrying the load alone. And it's saving this other company big dollars. Our offers are noncompetitive, but both are for female markets. Both of us are getting results."

Christine's promotional pieces ride with the book mailers. Postage costs go up a bit, but the makeup marketer covers that increase, plus half the other mailing expenses. In addition, she pays the book promoters a small commission on her sales. Everybody's happy.

Strategic alliances of that kind can be found through networking. Christine identified this interesting and fruitful cooperative effort by

- Watching mailers *she* received
- Attending local meetings of a direct marketing association

You should be able to locate firms that mail to markets similar to those you have targeted. Some of them would probably be open to including your mailing piece in their envelopes *if* they could benefit financially. As long as there is no competitive conflict, such a cooperative effort can indeed make a happy marriage.

Direct mail operators who are pressed for time, and need assistance in handling the myriad details of mailing, can use mailing services to great advantage. Here's how they work.

HOW MAILING SERVICE COMPANIES CAN SAVE YOU TIME AND MONEY

Mailing services are in the business of handling the vital steps involved in getting out a direct mail campaign. Leading services are prepared to take on client mailings as small as several hundred pieces to massive efforts of millions or more. A well-equipped service offers these support components:

- *Folding* in just about any format desired
- *Labeling* is the high-speed affixing of addresses on the mailing piece
- *Metering* of postage for virtually any size piece
- *Bursting* for separating forms, letters, and statements
- *Inserting* of contents into envelopes by machine

- *Handwork,* when required; the manual stuffing of envelopes

- *Collating* when various package elements have to be arranged in certain sequence

- *Mailing lists* for both consumer and business promotions (List maintenance by computer is also available in most instances.)

Many direct mail operators are initially dismayed at the magnitude of the task when they undertake preparation of even a modest sized mailing. They face hours of tedious manual labor and constantly struggle with the demands of getting every detail right in every single piece. A professional mailing service can eliminate those considerable headaches at modest cost. For example,

> One firm sends out 250 pieces per week and pays $45 to have a service do all the preparatory work. The client never sees the various components; after proofs are okayed, the printer ships all paper to the mailing service flat, and the completed mailing is on the way to prospects 24 hours later. This client saves *at least* six employee hours per week which amounts to $135, a savings of *$75 a week*.

A mailing service usually charges per 1,000 pieces, and the total amount depends on what kind of services are requested.

For big mailings, equipment can put address labels on envelopes at the rate of about 25,000 per hour. And quality is carefully watched.

Jan Romack, owner of JR Mailing Services in Bellevue, Washington, describes her services this way:

> "Most firms using direct mail, whether they're large or small, are ready to use a service after they have attempted to do their first mailing themselves. Getting it right, and doing it fast and economically, are the things a good service is set up to do.
>
> "Our clients' time is too valuable to spend on tedious manual work that we can do with fast, precise machines."

A top mailing service is also in a position to advise clients on every aspect of mailing, including the best paper weights to use, how to fold sheets, list acquisition, saving money on postage, and many other areas.

A word now about the best seasons to mail.

WATCHING THE SEASONS TO GET THE BEST BANG FOR YOUR DIRECT MAIL BUCK

To get the very most out of your direct marketing efforts, promote during fall and winter. This takes full advantage of holiday gift-giving times and the resulting consumer mood to purchase.

August through November marks the fall season, and December through March encompasses the winter season. In the winter period, sales of some products can slow from about mid-December through New Year's Day.

That is *not* to say all direct marketing efforts come to a halt from April through October. It's just that those spring and summer months do not generally produce as well. And it *is* safe to say that for most offers, July and August often turn out to be the doldrums in terms of response. This is largely due to heavy vacation schedules.

These good and not-so-good times to promote apply to *all* direct mail media. Here are two more strategies used by astute mail order firms.

DDB-1 AND DDB-2: TWO SUCCESS RECIPES FOR ANY MAIL ORDER COMPANY

DDB-1 and DDB-2 are not by any means new developments in direct mail. But they *were* refined and named by a respected direct mail marketing manager in a major U.S. publishing company. Here are descriptions of each program:

DDB-1: Dollar-Density Building

That simply means a successful mail order operation will *focus special promotional attention on consumers who are in a buying mood.*

In the words of one expert, the prime objective is to "Strike when the iron is hot." Parties who send in orders for various magazines and periodicals will *immediately* start to receive three or four times the normal number of mail contacts from this highly profitable company.

Such a stepped-up schedule works to increase the average customer expenditure some 45 percent over what it had been when buyers received normally spaced mailings. This manager says, "When the mood to purchase is there, *get the sales before somebody else does!*"

DDB-2: Drop Dormant Buyers

While intensified mailings go to hot buyers, the publishing firm takes a hard line on consumers and old customers who no longer respond.

If there is no activity from a consumer over a three-month time span, mailings are reduced from once every three months to twice a year. If six months pass without an order, a mailing goes out once a year. If a year goes by with no purchase, the name is dropped entirely after two years.

This firm is always searching new mailing lists for those active buyers, and is therefore reluctant to continue promoting to those who apparently are not interested.

A simple computer list maintenance system can tell you when prospects warrant increased or decreased promotional activity. More about that will be found in Chapter 7.

Next, consider a checklist that should help you keep a mailing campaign on track from start to finish.

DIRECT MAIL CHECKLIST

This checklist will help you create a direct mail program that's complete in every detail. It covers all the essential steps, from initial planning to evaluating program results.

Make copies of these pages, if you wish, and use the checklist *every time* you mail.

1. Basic Planning

In your initial direct mail planning, both the *overall program* and the *mailer itself* are considered. The very foundation of your direct mail effort should be based on this old and reliable "40/40/20" rule.

The success of your direct mail program hinges on the following elements:

Your choice of a market..............................40% importance

The impact of your offer ....40% importance

Quality of your creativity...........................20% importance

Therefore, your focus has to be on *list selection* and *putting together the best possible deal*. Following close behind is the *originality, clarity and "look" of your product or service presentation*.

While more time and energy goes into the foregoing three points, all the other important steps in the checklist definitely have to be addressed and worked out.

Answers that come out of your initial planning won't provide many definitive approaches, but certainly *should* give you solid guidelines to go by as you proceed through the checklist. Here are the basic planning steps:

Will your direct mail program be used to

_____ Sell products?   _____ Attract inquiries?

If selling is your objective, which product(s) and/or service(s) are to be sold?_____

_____

_____

_____

Have you worked out selling prices and profit margins?

_____ Yes   _____ No

Did you work out break-even figures and a budget for this campaign?

_____ Yes   _____ No

In addition to the basic offer, will you use special incentives to maximize sales?

_____ Yes   _____ No

Will you mail to

Consumers? _____ Businesses? _____

Describe as much as you can about the key characteristics of your ideal prospect: _____

_____

_____

Can lists of these prospects be readily obtained?

_____ Yes _____ No

How many prospects do you want to receive your mailing?

_____

Will you do some testing before you roll out your mailing program?

_____ Yes _____ No

Note the anticipated date of your mailing: _____

Describe the direct mail format you intend to use (envelope mailing, self-mailer, etc.): _____

_____

Who will handle the creative work such as copywriting, layout, and production of camera-ready boards? _____

_____

Have you identified several printers to bid on the project?

_____ Yes _____ No

Do you plan to use a mailing service that will coordinate folding, inserting, and other steps?

_____ Yes _____ No

Are you set up to handle fulfillment efficiently (products or information delivery)?

_____ Yes   _____ No

Notes:_____
_____
_____

2. List Selection

At this point, you want to get much more specific about *who* you'll be "talking" to in your campaign. Note: Review Chapter 7 before you complete this portion of the checklist.

Will your prospects have special expertise in the Product or service you are offering? (If so, that fact becomes essential when you specify a list).

_____ Yes   _____ No

List the zip codes you want to cover with your mailing:
_____

What kind of data should prospect listings include (specific name and title, address, phone number, etc.)? _____
_____

If you plan to test, describe which prospects you'll test (by zip codes, prospect type, or some other feature: _____
_____

How do you want listings to be provided to you (on labels, computer printout, etc.)? _____
_____

What's your budget for list acquisition? $ _____

Notes:_____

_____

_____

3. Offer

Now work out the all-important details of the offer. Note: Review Chapter 6 first. It may give you some effective tactics that can boost response.

Does your planned mailing date take full advantage of seasonal factors?

_____ Yes　　　_____ No

What action do you want prospects to take:

_____ Call an 800 number?

_____ Request additional information?

_____ Send an order and remittance?

_____ All of the above?

_____ Other: _____

If sales incentives are to be used, describe them here:

_____

Do all selected products and services fit the markets you have chosen?

_____ Yes   _____ No

Does your offer convey a genuinely good value?

_____ Yes   _____ No

Is your offer unique enough to attract prospect attention?

_____ Yes   _____ No

Notes:_____
_____
_____

4. Creative: Copy, Pictures, and Layout

List the vital points that have to be covered in descriptive copy: _____
_____
_____
_____

Consider using some of these elements to enhance the copy:

_____ Headlines

_____ Subheads

_____ Bullets

_____ Side bars

_____ Testimonials

Will you include copy about your guarantee terms?

_____ Yes   _____ No

Can your promotional piece be used to advantage for any other purpose, such as

_____ Trade show handouts

_____ Press release

_____ Package insert

_____ Other: _____

Will your format be an envelope mailer, a self-mailer, or some other? Describe: _____
_____

Describe your intended use of color in the printing process, if any: _____

Make *sure* that the layout for your mailer will

_____ Be *noticed*

_____ Be *opened*

_____ Be *read*

Notes:_____
_____
_____
_____

5. Order the List

Get assurance from your list broker on the following
points:

_____ The list has been maintained and is *at least*
90 percent deliverable.

_____ It has been compiled based on the prospect
characteristics you specified.

_____ It will be in your hands, in the correct format,
in time to meet your mailing schedule.

Notes:_____

_____

_____

6. Fulfillment

If literature (or some other kind of "additional information")
is promised, will it be ready in time for prompt fulfillment?

_____ Yes   _____ No

If product is to be sold or service is to be rendered, is it
ready to deliver?

_____ Yes   _____ No

Notes:_____

_____

_____

_____

7. Approval of Copy, Pictures, and Layout

Are you completely satisfied with *every* word of the copy, the quality of photos or illustrations, and the effectiveness of the layout?

_____ Yes _____ No

Notes:_____

_____

_____

8. Possession Of Lists

When lists are in your hands

_____ Double-check to see that the information you specified is in the listings

_____ Verify quantity of names

_____ Make sure list is provided in the format you ordered

Notes:_____

_____

_____

9. Camera-Ready Board Art Ready

Before taking to printer, check to see that all mailer inserts are present:

_____ Yes _____ No

Have boards been checked for total accuracy?

_____ Yes   _____ No

Are the correct photos or illustrations included?

_____ Yes   _____ No

Are all sizes as they should be?

_____ Yes   _____ No

If color is to be used, are instructions to the printer clear?

_____ Yes   _____ No

Notes:_____

_____

_____

10. Deliver Boards to Printer

Did you review all steps with the printer?

_____ Yes   _____ No

Is completion deadline agreed on?

_____ Yes   _____ No

Are all printing costs agreed on and documented?

_____ Yes   _____ No

Have you arranged to be present to check results when actual printing begins?

_____ Yes   _____ No

11. All Components to Mailing Service

Have you verfied correct quantities of all mailing package components?

_____ Yes   _____ No

Have you arranged to have all mailing components delivered to mailing service?

_____ Yes   _____ No

Have you reviewed with mailing service the correct processing of all components? Provide a sample of the desired finished mailer.

_____ Yes   _____ No

Have you set up a mailing deadline?

_____ Yes   _____ No

Notes:_____
_____
_____

12. Pay Postage

_____ Yes   _____ No

13. Mailing is Sent

_____ Yes   _____ No

14. Put in Place a System for Evaluating
Mailing Results

_____ Yes   _____ No

15. Follow-up

Describe your plan for recontacting prospects who did not purchase: _____
_____

16. Describe the Approach You'll
Use to Resell Buyers:

_____
_____
_____
_____

Notes:_____
_____
_____

CHAPTER 6

MAIL ORDER POWER-SELLING TACTICS

A leather backpack would undoubtedly appeal to lots of mail order buyers merely on the strength of its durability and appearance. But when the same product is presented as a replica of the backpack carried by 1930s roving reporters, sales may well go into orbit.

Still bigger sales might be rung up if a matching checkbook cover was offered as a special free premium.

This chapter is about the romance and merchandising tactics that magically turn ordinary mail order offers into spectacular winners without much extra effort.

ROMANCE: THE MOST POWERFUL SELLER OF ALL

John Hinterberger, a *Seattle Times* staff columnist, recently wrote about mail order romance. He quoted this copy from the J. Peterman Co. mail order catalog, selling a 1939-style linen blouse:

"They were young.

"They met at a party in London.

"They made each other laugh. They fell in love.

"After the party, they walked. In a shop window they saw a linen blouse. It was simple and beautiful, and he wanted to buy it for her. But it was Sunday.

"A week later, war was declared.

"He was called up immediately...

99

"He was gone a year, then two years. London was being bombed
nightly. She waited for news. The radio was never off. The news
was never good.

The copy then describes her loneliness, the war's end, her search
for that same blouse, and finally an emotional reunion with her
long-absent love:

"They got a seat on the train to London. By the time they got there,
a little laughing was starting to come."

Then the blouse itself is described in the copy, followed by,

"Same blouse she wore the day he came back. Sizes 8, 10, 12, 14.
Price $94."

Pure romance. This approach is exceptionally effective in building mystique around a product, making it fun to buy—and giving it
a feeling of being more unusual than it really is. Would the same
blouse on a department store shelf *ever* convey that kind of glamor?
Not a chance.

Mr. Peterman says, "People want things that are hard to find.
Things that have romance."

Of course it's entirely true that kitchen tools, plastic decorative
items, vegetable seeds, and other relatively mundane mail order
products are more difficult to romanticize. But to some degree *it is
possible to go further than simply developing dull, factual copy*. To
do so requires some research, imagination, and a little flair. But the
end result will be more dramatic, and *far* more effective at selling
merchandise and services. For example,

- Why can't an ordinary kitchen tool be described as the same
  style as one used by an aunt in Rome who has relied on it for
  decades to prepare fabulous arrays of mouth-watering
  delicacies?

- Is it possible that a plastic decoration may be modeled after
  a priceless Grecian urn unearthed during an 1886 archae-
  ological expedition?

- Could the copy for packages of bean seeds suggest that the
  plants might climb into the sky like Jack's fabled beanstalk?

Good fiction is all it is. These romantic tidbits do not promise
better performance or superior quality. Just simply more fun for the
buyer.

While some of us may be able to resist romance of that sort, few can turn away from something *free*.

FREE OFFERS THAT CLOSE THE TOUGHEST CUSTOMERS

There are precious few consumers who actually believe that a free gift is really free. Today's more sophisticated shopper can't see a supplier passing up a chunk of profit to cover the cost of a no-charge premium. Most people are convinced that the profit slack created by a free gift is taken up by other products sold at slightly higher prices. They are more often than not correct.

Yet, amazingly, people still respond to "free" gift offers in huge numbers. It's one of the best available mail order gimmicks for pushing a procrastinator over the edge toward a purchase and for unloading slow sellers; a gift will help sales of lagging products. The buyer's feeling that he or she is getting the advantage in the transaction overpowers the stark reality that the gift isn't free at all.

Free gift offers come in several interesting forms. Here are a few of the possibilities:

- One promoter of fashion accessories occasionally permits catalog shoppers to select any one item in its book at no cost if it's of the same or lesser dollar value than the total of items purchased at the regular price.

  Such a deal is definitely generous, and this mail order merchandiser most certainly does take a hit on profit margin. To help ease the pain, customers are asked to pay a $2.50 handling charge on the free item. Buyers don't bat an eye at the charge since their gift generally carries a retail of at least $24.99.

- "Two-for-one" offers are essentially free gift deals. *Buy one, get a second one free* works successfully for a San Francisco mail order firm in media ads.

- A gift product mailing company presents a free item in every one of its campaigns. The give-away generally costs the promoter $1.00 to $3.00. Free gifts have included cheese board/knife sets, candy dishes, and glass paperweights. The low-cost free items selected by this firm are *always* in the gift category, so their customers invariably like them.

Any size purchase is shipped with the give-away provided the customer checks it off on the order form and agrees to pay 75 cents handling.

- Perhaps the all-time classic free gift offer is one that has been used by book clubs for decades. Subscribe to club membership and select a number of books for a sum that anybody knows would barely cover postage and handling. Retail value of the initial book shipment is clearly $50 or more, so the deal is credible and compelling.

This marvelously successful book promotion can be described as the perfect "loss leader," covered next in more detail.

USING LEADERS TO TRIGGER THE BUYING RESPONSE

Leaders are items of *established* retail value available at steeply reduced prices. For example,

- A top-name 700/800/1,500-watt quartz heater/humidifier with two steam settings and tip-over switch. $59.95. *Only $19.00* while supplies last!

Remember, a leader has to be a ***bonafide, easily recognized bargain.*** If the brand name can be shown in the promotion—and it's a respected, quality-oriented manufacturer—by all means print that name in a prominent spot. A leader can *fail* to stir up consumer interest if people perceive the item as an obscure brand of questionable value.

Merchandisers fully expect to make just a little money on the leader itself, but count on other purchases to absorb the shortfall. Wise shoppers who have a need for the heater will instantly recognize the outstanding value and consequently make the decision to buy the unit. At the same time, they may very well order other needed or wanted items. The point is, leaders tend to get shoppers into a buying mode. Here's one of the reasons why that happens:

A big splash in an ad or mailer creates a "bargain psychology." A strong leader can establish an atmosphere of wishful thinking that makes all items around the leader look like great deals, whether they are or not.

As would be expected, some savvy consumers order *only* the leader. Some merchants call these buyers "cherry-pickers." While a transaction like that brings a loss to the merchandiser, it can serve the valuable purpose of adding a new customer who will buy at regular prices in the future. And leaders help hold the interest of past customers.

Losses that accompany leaders are recovered by mail order operators in these interesting ways:

- A "razor blade" situation can be beautifully built through leader merchandising. Sell the razor itself at an extremely low price, and its owner will buy fresh blades from you at high profit for years to come. This principle is used by a mail order tool marketer. He sells a ratchet plus a few basic socket attachments at a leader price. Then he offers scores of accessories at their regular price. Of course, the accessories will only fit the ratchet.

- "First-in-a-set" also lends itself to leader selling by mail order. The product line is a set of 12 beautiful ceramic mugs with pictures of one exotic automobile on each piece. The initial two mugs are offered for just pennies each, but subsequent matching releases go for the regular price of $6.95 each. About half of the leader buyers want to complete their set. Overall profit is very healthy.

Please note: In promoting a leader for a first-in-a- set offer, don't forget to make it clear in your copy that prices on later releases will be at regular retail levels!

As effective as these leader programs are, here's one that is used more widely and successfully than any other.

STEP-UPS CAN DOUBLE YOUR INCOMING CASH

Probably the oldest merchandising tactic, step-ups, never seem to lose their selling punch. They can be seen in any good mail order catalog and retail outlet.

To handle a step-up correctly, your first move is to identify a leader. In this case, start with an item that is *not* top of the line, but rather a basic model that has deluxe big brothers. Your objective is to attract consumer attention with price and then get the shopper involved in a more substantial model at a slightly higher price. Using small appliances as an example, a good step-up program might look like the microwave ovens in Figure 6-1:

Figure 6-1. "Step-Ups" Using the Long–Successful "Good, Better, Best"

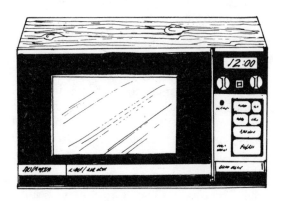

A. Excellent MICROWAVE OVEN
Two power levels, defrost and turntable features.
"Easy touch" keypad controls. 30-minute timer, 500 watts.
Only 26 lbs. ONLY $110

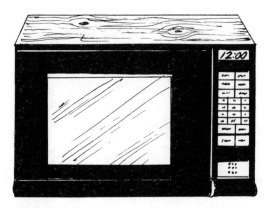

B. Outstanding MICROWAVE OVEN
Three-stage memory, auto weight defrost and turntable.
Big one-cubic-foot capacity, 650 watts and 99-minute timer.
Solid 36 lbs. ONLY $139

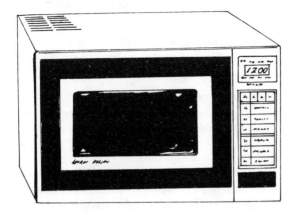

C. Superb CONVECTION/MICROWAVE OVEN
Gourmet's choice. Four-stage memory, five power levels, 99-minute timer, and spacious 1.2 cubic foot capacity. Powerful 700 watts of power. Defrost and turntable.
A substantial 60 lbs. ONLY $269

Consumers will be drawn to the $110 leader. But the shopper's attention should quickly turn to the "outstanding" oven that costs only $29 more than the basic model and boasts some features the leader does not have. Even the additional 10 lbs. heft of the step-up helps to establish a story of higher quality.

Many shoppers will switch themselves to B, the better product, which carries a decent profit. A smaller percentage of consumers will decide to go all out and select C, a truly top-of-the-line appliance. Sears has extensively used a "good/better/best" presentation on products ranging from bedding to power lawn mowers.

Please note that illustrations or photos will rarely convey the enhanced value of "better" over "good" or "best" over "better." That story has to be established in the *descriptive copy*.

The most important success components in an effective step-up program are

- To work out the smallest possible price spread between the leader and step-up. When the dollar increase is minimal, shoppers will more readily jump up a notch to the better,

higher-priced product. A wide difference will defeat the
purpose of the program.

- To set up the program so you break even or lose a few cents
  on the leader, but profit on the step-up. The leader *has to
  be dramatically priced*.

- To identify and describe features in the step-up that do not
  exist in the leader. For each move up in quality, there
  should be more to say in your copy about product capability.

It seems that three or more step-ups work better than just having
a leader and *one* step-up. Perhaps the comparative quality of the *best*
item in the group makes the leader look even more basic than it really
is and the step-up a solid compromise.

More money-making ideas follow.

MORE MERCHANDISING TACTICS THAT BRING IN BIG SALES

By *asking for action, creating urgency,* or both, a mail order offer will
pack more punch. The following tactics will *not* increase your risk,
but do help attract attention:

- *Yes/No* powerfully involves your prospect in the buying
  decision. Tests have proven that response increases when
  the reader of an ad or mailer is requested to act on a yes or
  no verdict and then inform you as to which answer was
  arrived at. Typical wording in a promotion like this might
  read

- YES! I am ordering at this time.

- NO, not this time. But keep me in mind when your new
  selections are available.

Asking your prospect to check one of the boxes is the simplest
version of a yes/no offer. It can be enhanced by providing a small
sticker that the prospect presses onto the yes or no box, such as the
one pictured in Figure 6-2. This rendition of the yes/no offer *is* more
costly to produce, but adds fun and involvement.

**Figure 6-2. This High-Energy Mailer Has Four Adhesive Stickers
To Get Prospect Involvement!**

While "no" responses don't bring in immediate sales, they do provide valuable clues about which names on your mailing list might be worth following up. At least you know they're reading your piece!

- *Time Limits* create urgency and therefore help stir procrastinators into action.

To make a time limit work, you have to be reasonably certain about the delivery date of your mailer, the publication date of your print ad, or the air date of your broadcast spots. Allow sufficient time for response; 30-days can work well for most offers. Avoid long time limits since that tends to take the urgency out of the offer.

If at all possible, use a *specific deadline date* instead of a period of time, like this:

ORDER *TODAY* . . . THIS REMARKABLE VALUE IS AVAIL-ABLE *ONLY* UNTIL MONDAY, SEPTEMBER 20!

or

ORDER *TODAY* . . . ON MONDAY, SEPTEMBER 20 THIS IN-CREDIBLE HERBAL TEA SAMPLER COLLECTION GOES BACK TO $19.95!

* *Optional terms* give your prospect an incentive to make a bigger commitment because you offer a better buy when larger quantities are ordered. This is similar to the quantity discount merchants can take when they agree to buy in volume. One catalog operator does it this way:

If your order is . . .

$19.99 to $29.99, take an additional 5% DISCOUNT

$30.00 TO $39.99, take an additional 10% DISCOUNT

$40.00 or more, take an additional 15% DISCOUNT

A fascinating variation of optional terms is now described.

HOW TO PRESENT THE "DO-EVEN-BETTER" MULTIPLE-UNIT PRICE BREAK

Figure 6-3 illustrates a successful media ad strategy used by a West Coast–based mail order company.

Figure 6-3. How to Present the "Do-Even-Better" Deal

VCR ENHANCER
Only $39.85*
*But read the ad for an even better deal!

After detailed descriptive copy, the following paragraph in the Haverhills ad provides detail on how the better deal works:

Buy Two for $79.90, and we'll send you a third one, with our compliments—absolutely FREE

This innovative firm has featured a variety of products in its do-even-better program. It's nothing less than amazing that so many buyers purchase as many as *three identical products* in order to get a steep price break. But the fact is, people buy for friends, employees, and business associates. It *works* beyond any shadow of a doubt.

Any of the sales-building techniques described so far in this chapter can be used in combination with others. For example, why *not* use the yes/no tactic with a leader/step-up promotion? And why wouldn't a time limit work with optional terms? In truth, the more excitement you can pack into your promotions, the better they will do. Use the worksheet at the end of the chapter to help work out a mixture of tactics for your next promotion.

Each of the tactics described can be used at absolutely *no risk* by a direct marketer who can't afford to lose money. They are effective but entirely safe. Here are some tactics that also work, but do have the potential to lose money and credibility.

Gimmicks to Avoid if You're Just Starting Out

In getting off to a strong start in a mail order business of your own, the *last* thing you need is a program that puts you in jeopardy of losing precious cash or consumer goodwill. This section takes you through a few of the merchandising tactics that *are* used effectively by big, well-financed firms, but could make a small operator extremely vulnerable to reverses.

- *Contests* can be phenomenally successful, but are horrendously tricky for these reasons: Federal Trade Commission (FTC) regulations governing contests are tough. Also, you'd need a massive promotional budget to make this tactic work. One case that illustrates the potential for disaster occurred recently when a huge food company's printer turned out *hundreds* of coupons that entitled holders to a new car, when only one vehicle was available. The firm was besieged with lawsuits. For right now, leave contests to the giant merchandisers.

- *Lifetime memberships* require an up-front fee from the buyer. That fee entitles this individual to special pricing forevermore. Trouble is, how do you define a "lifetime"?

Is it transferable to another family member? And *whose* lifetime are we talking about, the customer's or the vendor's? This is a gimmick loaded with potential hard feelings and possible litigation.

- *Til forbid* provides for automatic shipments to customers on a prearranged basis. For example, in a collection of 12 die-cast classic auto models, 1 is to be delivered every month at $29.95 each until the collection is all shipped—or until the customer tells the supplier to stop.

  This technique is viable for a new mail order firm *if* a sophisticated fulfillment system is in place and if the company is assured of getting the right products at the right times so deliveries remain precisely on schedule.

- *Negative option* means that the customer has to take action to refuse or return a delivery or else pays for the product or service. These mailings can be downright offensive to consumers. In one case, a firm offers an appointment book for the coming year at a conspicuously low price. In small print, the offer explains that *next year's* book will automatically be sent in 12 months and billed at the considerably higher retail price.

Figure 6-4 shows the merchandise return label enclosed with the later, negative option merchandise delivery:

- A great many consumers *will* return the product shipped a whole year later because they have forgotten, or never saw, the small print in the original offer. These consumers discover they have to pay return postage, plus a merchandise return fee, if the item is not wanted. A huge number will simply keep the product, thinking it's an unsolicited product mailing (which they *can* legally do).

  Risks to the shipper are enormous in negative option programs, and FTC guidelines have to be carefully watched due to past abuses by promoters.

Now we'll cover some power-selling ideas that are not actually part of the offer itself, but can be routinely included in *every* promotion you create in order to boost response.

Figure 6-4. Merchandise Return Label Used in a
Negative Option Promotion

INSTRUCTIONS FOR RETURNING MERCHANDISE
**FOLLOWING THIS PROCEDURE WILL ELIMINATE
THE NEED TO CALL CUSTOMER SERVICE**

1. Fill out this card, detach, and enclose it with merchandise.
2. Adhere Merchandise Return Label (below) to package before mailing (no postage necessary).

IMPORTANT!

All books must be returned within 30 days of receipt. If you have been billed for the book(s), a credit for your returned merchandise will appear on a subsequent billing statement.

Date_____ Please Check One: ___ Replace ___ Credit My Account
Titles or Descriptions
of Book(s) Being Returned_____

Other Comments
or Instructions_____

Name_____

Address_____

City_____ State _____ Zip _____

Order Number_____
      (see carton label)

3645

DETACH HERE

FROM _____
_____
_____
ACCEPTANCE POST OFFICE FOR
ANCILLARY SERVICES ONLY
    POSTAGE _____
MERCHANDISE RETURN FEE ___.20___
INSURANCE FEE IF ANY ___0___
TOTAL POSTAGE DUE $_____

(See 919.6 Domestic Mail Manual)

DELIVERY POST OFFICE
COMPUTE POSTAGE DUE
(See 919.7 DOMESTIC MAIL
MANUAL)

**BOUND
PRINTED
MATTER**

NO POSTAGE
NECESSARY
IF MAILED
IN THE
UNITED STATES

MERCHANDISE RETURN LABEL
PERMIT #4   NEBRASKA 68114
OMAHA   352 N 76th St.

POSTAGE DUE UNIT
U.S. POSTAL SERVICE
OMAHA, NE 68114

DISPELLING THE THREE MAIN BUYER ANXIETIES

Customer comfort and confidence sells as much merchandise, and perhaps more, than low prices. If you can assure buyers that you are a safe, reliable source, a sale is *far* more likely to come your way. There are three major anxieties that have to be settled in any successful mail order offer. They are:

- **Vendor trust.** Does the shopper have sufficient faith that your company will deliver what is promised in promotions? In the eyes of skeptical prospects, the firm making a mail order offer is all too often guilty until proven innocent. So special steps must be taken to create trust. This is doubly important when the consumer glances at your promotion for the very first time.

- **Is the offer a good value?** Very few mail order offers are obvious good values. Price/quality comparisons are seldom available to your prospects. For example, is the $19.95 plastic freezer container set on a par with the one displayed at the supermarket? A potential buyer has no choice but to believe your descriptive copy and hope the price is in line for the quality offered.

- **Is the choice prudent?** Virtually every mail order buyer goes through doubt as to the wisdom of the selection. Will the plastic containers fit the available freezer space? Will each item really be functional? Are they needed in the first place?

All the hype, dazzling copy, and free gifts in creation will fall short of dispelling those buyer anxieties. It takes a powerful customer assurance program to blow those consumer apprehensions out of the path of a purchase. Here's an array of approaches that *will* go a long way toward putting your buyers at ease.

LITTLE-KNOWN CUSTOMER ASSURANCE PROGRAMS THAT HELP EVAPORATE BUYER RESISTANCE

In a totally solid mail order program, all six of these customer assurance facets should be present to help allay buyer fears:

- **Free trial or unconditional money-back guarantee.** In either case, your customer will be shielded from all major anxieties since the sale can be nullified with no loss whatsoever to the consumer.

  A free trial is the stronger of the two since there is *no* payment until the product or service is used by the buyer.

Of course, risk to the mail order operator is considerably higher in this instance.

Effectiveness of an unconditional money-back guarantee still relies to some extent on trust of the consumer since the order is paid for in advance, and a customer may wonder if the refund will, in fact, be honored by the seller. Federal regulations require *every* mail order firm to refund a prompt merchandise return, so the money-back offer is really not an act of extra generosity, but simply conformity with law.

Please see Chapter 8 for examples of extremely effective guarantees you can use.

- *Prompt response to customers.* Questions like "Where's my free gift?" "Can I get the napkin holders in green?" and "Will the bookends be available in January?" will arrive in a flow roughly proportional to the amount of business being handled by a mail order company.

  Higher-volume mail order operators use word processing to quickly cover the most frequently asked questions. A big mail order firm created a library of computerized response letters over a period of years and today can handle an average of *200 customer questions per day* on an 8-hour turnaround basis.

  If you can't handle computerization right now, develop preprinted form letters that can be used to provide answers rapidly to your customers. You'll find sample letters in Chapter 10.

- *Customer-only promotions.* If you can obtain outstanding buys on smaller quantities of products, you're in an ideal position to put together a customer-only offer. Such a mailing has to look like a superbonus and is strictly limited to prior buyers. It's an extremely flattering event to those who patronize you. Two customer-only sales per year are about right. If you run too many of them, they start to look like business as usual.

- *Seasonal greetings* can consist of one "We Wish You a Happy Holiday Season" card during the Christmas/New

Year's season. This simple but tasteful card doesn't sell anything and should not express any religious meaning since you can't be certain about customer preferences. Send this card alone. It loses something if it's enclosed with a promotion.

- *Telephone contact with key customers.* A consistently large-volume buyer warrants a couple of your valuable minutes. When an individual like this gets a call from you, he or she will definitely feel special.

  Be sure to call at a time when heavy buying *is underway*. If you call *after* purchases have started to slack off, your contact resembles just another effort to win back lost business. Basic content of the call is built around these points:

We're delighted you like our selection.

Do you find everything you need?

Is everything we send up to your expectations?

Please let me know *personally* if we can do anything for you.

When you build those important customer satisfaction measures into your mail order program, you will establish customer trust and credibility at a rapid rate, and your sales will reflect the growing goodwill.

Now, consider the following tools for boosting sales.

FULFILLMENT "RIDE-ALONGS" CAN DOUBLE YOUR MAIL ORDER SALES

Any merchandise or service delivery you make is virtually wasted *if it doesn't include a new promotion*. Ride-alongs, sometimes known as "bounce-backs," are based on the theory that somebody who just bought from you is the best possible prospect.

Ride-alongs can be enclosed in invoices, routine correspondence, *and* merchandise shipments. The most powerful aspect of this is *postage is absolutely free*.

Ideally, a ride-along will do best if the recipient hasn't seen it in your other promotions. Some companies withhold selected items from their mainstream promotions and use them exclusively for ride-along exposure.

You can be *certain* that a consumer who orders from you, and then receives your delivery, will *open* that package and carefully review all the contents. So ride-alongs *do get seen* by consumers who have already demonstrated their trust for you and your products. There can be *no* better prospect than that.

As many as five or six ride-alongs can accompany the packages and other correspondence you send out to customers. If this selection is related in some way to the delivered product, all the better. Corky Langner promotes sports products by mail. Every delivery made to a customer includes a special circular offering various how-to books on sports. These high-profit publications account for some 40 percent of Corky's annual sales.

Whether you sell by mail, media ads, television, or radio, make sure that every order you deliver contains a promotion!

Would you pay a dollar and change to get a big increase in your mail order sales? An entrepreneur in Oregon happily does it about 20 times a week.

TEMPTING DELIVERY INCENTIVES THAT CAN DRAMATICALLY BOOST PURCHASE DOLLARS

When Jon Wallace offered free delivery on any gift order of $20 or more, he couldn't believe how quickly his average sale increased. Consumers immediately started adding items onto their orders to save an average of $1.80 in postage and handling.

"It works because I still charge $1.80 postage and handling for any order up to $19.99. Lots of buyers who select a $17 or $18 total start searching for another item costing $5 to $10 so they can get over that $20 level. They figure the additional purchase will automatically cost $1.80 less—the amount they'll save on postage.

"That little change to my mailers increased my average sale from $18.06 to $29.90. Shipping the larger order costs me only about $2, so the profit remains very healthy."

Bev Stark markets art supplies by mail. She offers one of three free gifts to any buyer spending $30 or more. Her average sale went up $12.65 as soon as this new program was introduced. Giving buyers a little incentive to raise the size of their order is plain good business sense. A Midwest-based food specialty marketer pointed out the method he used to develop an incentive for raising his average sale:

> "Our first step was to make absolutely sure about the dollar volume of an average order. After tracking figures carefully for a year, we found the amount was exactly $56. From that point, we identified a *desired* average sale that we could reasonably reach. We decided on $75—an increase of $19."

The point is, you *don't* want to create incentives until you know where your average sale is *now* and where you *want it to be*. Set the increase at *a reachable level*.

In some mail order firms, the use of 900 telephone lines can be tremendous revenue generators. We'll explore that area now.

HOW 900 PHONE LINES CAN MAKE YOU BIG MONEY

A growing number of astute marketers are wondering why so many companies give away so much valuable information. In this exploding age of information, it's a *must* for every company to take a new look at the sales appeal of the knowledge it possesses.

If *you* have information that buyers want, or something else of value, selling that know-how through a 900 line can lead you to the easiest profits imaginable. For example,

- An East Coast firm that publishes a much wanted product catalog takes requests for the book by 900 line. In addition to getting its wares into the hands of hot buyers, it *makes money on each call*.

- A firm that deals in financial referrals handles its customers almost exclusively by 900 line. It's a formidable profitmaker for them.

Firms using 900 lines dispense information to prospects and customers alike. There are legal hotlines, tech-tip services, and other advisory sources in action via the 900 route. One company charges *$50 per minute* for advice from an expert, although more typical 900 charges are about $2 for the first minute, and $1 or less for each additional minute.

You'll make about two-thirds of the amount billed to callers. If you lease computerized call-directing equipment, expect your profit to be around 50 percent of the amount billed to callers. Local exchange companies like U.S. West take care of billing callers and transferring the proceeds to the 900 line holder.

You've probably experienced computerized systems. They have the capability of answering calls this way:

- "For personal assistance in placing an order, please press '1.'"

- "For a copy of our free catalog, please press '2.'"

- "To contact our service department, press '3.'"

Since 900 calls come into a firm's regular telephone lines, there are rarely if ever busy signals or waits on hold. You can set your service up so a recorded voice informs the caller about the per minute charge you have set so there are no surprises when your customer receives his or her phone bill.

Al Massena, an account executive with AT&T's Business Marketing Group, explained that the cost of 900 service is $1,200 per month. This cost can be reduced if a firm shares 900 service and costs with one or more other companies. When such an arrangement is made, the 900 line holder can of course mark up the charges to profit yet another way.

Low or no-cost public relations will almost always increase the results of your mail order promotional programs. Here's how it can be done.

GETTING VALUABLE FREE PUBLICITY

Whatever you do, *don't* overlook free publicity for your mail order business! Hundreds of extra buyers would gladly patronize you if they knew you existed. One very good way to let them know about your business is via local publications of various types. You can send out announcements under a specially prepared letterhead like the one in Figure 6-5:

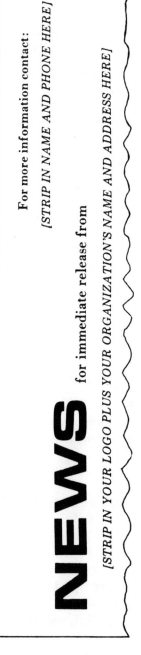

Figure 6-5. News Release Letterhead

Your press release should be done in journalistic style, more "newsy" than "salesy." The two- or three-line heading you put at the top of this release is your best chance to summarize the importance of your product, catalog, or whatever else you decide to announce. This heading is the key to getting your point across.

For example:

Unique Italian Office Gadgets are Functional
And Dramatic Style-Setters

Neighborhood newspapers almost always want to print items about interesting developments. Many of them would consider the starting of a new business—or the introduction of a new product or service— worthy of free space.

One way to get the attention of newspapers is to come up with a genuinely unusual product. Don't worry if it has limited appeal; its *real* value will be in its newsworthiness. Provide a photograph of the product, and of yourself.

One other excellent possibility for free publicity lies in the area of churches, organizations, and clubs. They are extremely active in fund raising activities. These functions almost always require the donation of gifts. When you make such donations, you can usually get your money's worth of publicity in newsletter, bulletins, or other types of house organs.

One more good idea is a gift give-away program through the same organizations just mentioned. Many groups like this try to assist families during the Christmas season. They collect and distribute items to those who are in need of a little happiness. If you are in a position to award a group of products to an organization in your area, it can service the dual purpose of helping people and bringing you important recognition.

To help you pull the best mail order merchandising tactics together in an integrated powerhouse of a program, use the work-sheet that follows.

WORKSHEET FOR PLANNING YOUR MAIL ORDER ATTACK

This worksheet summarizes the best low-risk power selling tactics available. The more compatible tactics you can pack into each promotion, the harder they will sell. Make as many copies of the worksheet pages as you need, and use them for *every* promotion.

Free Gift Offer

Your customer can pick a free item when a purchase is made at regular price.

Select *one* of the following free gift approaches for this promotion:

☐   *Version 1:* Customer can choose any item you offer that has a retail value *equal to* or *less than* the value of items purchased at regular prices.

☐   *Version 2:* Customer can choose one *preselected* free gift shown in your promotion.

Answer these questions regarding the version you selected for this promotion:

If version 2, is there a minimum purchase amount that has to be reached to qualify for free gift?

Do you plan to charge your customer postage and handling for the free gift?

_____ Yes _____ No

Describe other details of your free gift offer:_____

_____

_____

Leader and Step-Up

If you elect to offer a free gift, you may not want to use a leader as well. If you *do* use both, make very sure your profit margins will be sufficient.

Select *one* of the following leader approaches for this promotion:

☐　*Version 1: First-in-a-Step.* Customer can order the initial item of a set at reduced price

☐　*Version 2: Leader and Set-up* (good, better, best).

Answer these questions about the version you selected for this promotion

If first-in-a-set, describe how you'll price both the
initial item and subsequent items:_____
_____

Will your customers be required to order later releases
in the set (negative option technique), or will you automatically ship and bill them? Describe: _____
_____

What time interval will you have between releases? __
_____
_____

Are certain that *all* items in the set will be available
when you need them?

_____ Yes　　　_____ No

If your selected leader and step-up for this promotion,
describe the leader and step-up:

Leader:_____
_____

Your cost: $_____   Retail price: $_____

Step 1:_____

_____

Your cost: $_____   Retail price: $_____

Step 2:_____

_____

Your cost: $_____   Retail price: $_____

Request for Action

Customer is requested to make a yes or no choice to
your offer.

Select one of the following methods:

☐   Customer is to check a yes or no box on your
     order form.

☐   Mailer provides a self-adhesive disk that custo-
     mer places on the yes or no box before return-
     ing to you.

☐   In addition to yes/no boxes, will you provide a
     third choice, such as "Send me more informa-
     tion"? If so, describe: _____

     _____

Urgency

Time limit. Customer can get the offered value only if
the order is submitted on or before a specified date.

When will your promotion reach prospects? _____

_____

What response deadline will you specify? _____

_____

Incentives to Increase Order Size

☐ *Optional terms.* Customer gets free delivery if dollar amount of order exceeds a certain level.

At what dollar level will postage and handling be given free? $ _____

☐ *Do-even-better.* Customer gets a price break if more than one of *the same item* is ordered.

Describe how discounts will work on second and third items: _____

_____

☐ *Extra discounts on larger orders.* You may decide *not* to use both the do-even-better and the extra discount tactics in the same promotion.

List price brackets and corresponding discount percentages:

If total order exceeds $_____, take an additional _____% discount.

If total order is between $_____ and $_____, take an additional _____% discount.

If total order is between $_____$ and $_____$,
take an additional $_____$ % discount.

If total order is between $_____$ and $_____$,
take an additional $_____$ % discount.

Fulfillment Ride-Alongs (Bounce-Backs)

Select *one* of these mail order policies:

☐ *Version 1: Free trial.* Customer is given a definite pe-
    riod of time to try your product or service before pay-
    ment is required.

☐ *Version 2: Unconditional money-back guarantee.* Custo-
    mer pays for order in advance, but is given a reason-
    able length of time to return the order for a refund.

Describe terms for the version you selected: $_____$
_____
_____
_____
_____

Publicity Planned for This Promotion

Describe efforts to be made in getting free press exposure for this offer: _____
_____
_____

Notes: _____
_____
_____
_____

CHAPTER 7

LIST BUILDING: THE VITAL CORNERSTONE OF *ANY* MAIL ORDER PROGRAM

By far, the most asked question from new mail order operators is; "Where can I get the best list?" It's as if there's a broker or directory somewhere that will provide perfect prospects, in precisely the correct quantities, in just the right locations. The facts are:

> Successful mail order firms spend more time and energy on list building and list maintenance than on any other aspect of their operations. And that effort *never stops*. It's a vital, continuing program that can and does *pay enormous dividends*.

There are no deep, dark secrets about lists. The answers you need are *in this chapter*.

WHY A GOOD LIST IS BY FAR YOUR MOST POWERFUL ASSET

A department store with thousands of active, loyal customers can *count on* an ongoing flow of sales and steady growth through referrals. An auto dealership that has sold a certain make of car in the community over a period of years will get repeat buyers for new models far into the future.

In both cases, the firms spent their early years getting the word out to consumers. Gradually a customer base was established. Then a pattern started to take shape as to who the customers were. Both companies began to understand more about where buyers lived, how much they earned, and what kinds of life-styles they preferred. Both organizations learned how to find more of these "right" buyers.

At the same time, the nucleus of previous buyers had to be tracked. People moved and married. Kids reached ages where they became customers in their own right, as their parents slowed down as spenders.

There is really *no difference whatsoever* between the customer-building procedure and the process used by prosperous direct marketers. If anything at all has changed, it's that list building is easier today than it was when the department store and auto dealership started. There are two reasons for this:

1. Computers can compile list data in a matter of hours that a decade ago took days or weeks.

2. We know more about demographics now. It's a simple matter to specify the kind of consumer or business prospects we want and *get* them in quantity, with reasonable accuracy.

Unlike the two firms in the preceding example, *you* can build a valuable customer list with remarkable speed *by following a series of proven steps.* An interesting case study in finding list sources is now described.

IDENTIFYING *ALL* THE BEST LIST SOURCES

A U.S. company in the Southwest selling business systems to medical offices put together an effective list-building strategy to prepare for its first direct mail campaign. The steps it took in setting up its successful program started with identifying sources of company names. Roy Knowlton, the firm's vice president of marketing, describes the process:

> "Our task was somewhat simplified since we wanted to mail to every medical office we possibly could in a four-state area, and medical companies are not that tough to spot. Our big challenge was, we realized it would take many sources to build a good list."

These sources were identified as the best ones available:

- Yellow Pages. Medical offices have to be highly visible to consumers, so the classified telephone book is where they can be found in abundance.

- AMA (American Medical Association) and ADA (American Dental Association) directories.

- Hospital staff lists.

- University graduation lists.

- New business licenses.

- Newspaper announcements, regarding new office openings.

- Chamber of Commerce directory.

- Health Maintenance Organizations (HMO) groups.

- Personal observation during routine travels.

"After we collected all the company names from each list, the task of eliminating duplicates had to be done. This 'merge/purge' operation was accomplished on a personal computer. Ongoing maintenance of our new list is by far the most crucial job we face. One person in our company is charged with the chore of cleaning the list on a weekly basis."

Some companies, like Roy Knowlton's firm, build their own lists. In his case, the market was easy to identify, the prospect sources fairly obvious, and the targeted geographical area relatively small. The compiling task in this case was as straightforward as it could possibly be. But for most direct mailers, the services of a reputable list house are strongly advised.

IMPORTANT INFORMATION ABOUT LIST HOUSES

Under the heading Mailing Lists in most big-city classified telephone directories, you'll find a rich selection of list companies. Some are branch offices of national organizations, others are local firms. As in any industry, most are sophisticated, knowledgeable, and accommodating, but a few are not much more than quick-buck artists.

Virtually any list house is prepared to offer you two different kinds of mailing lists:

1. *Compiled lists* are put together from public records such as tax records, home sales, census data, warranty responses, and even ordinary telephone books.

Anybody who devotes enough time to the task can compile a list. Roy Knowlton did exactly that from the sources listed earlier in this chapter. He succeeded in capturing virtually every medical office in a four-state area, but he had no way of knowing how big those offices were, or who the buyer was. The data on compiled lists are very basic.

Compiled lists are low cost and offer huge numbers of names. For example, there are some *14 million business firms* available on compiled lists in the United States.

2. *Mail order responder (proprietary) lists* are simply the customer lists of firms that have decided to rent them out for a little extra income. You can get *known* mail order buyers of spices or camping equipment, commercial aviators, political candidates, or practically any other specialized category if you shop around enough.

A broker who rents proprietary lists will want to make sure you aren't promoting products competitive to the wares of the list owner, and almost certainly will ask to review your mailer to make sure it's in good taste.

Proprietary lists are considerably more costly than are compiled lists and are subject to more restrictions. As a case in point, some list owners will tell their broker that a renter is prohibited from calling their customers. And some will permit only one contact by mail for the rental fee. Brokers will often seed their client's list with the names of aunts, sons, and cousins so they can find out when restrictions are violated.

Virtually all list owners realize that when they rent out their customer lists, merchandise and services will be sold to some of their patrons. When that happens, the names of those who buy can no longer be held in a restricted category by the original list owner; when you sell a prospect on a list you rent, that name belongs to you.

A good list broker can act as a consultant to a direct marketer by reviewing list demographics and your products to help assure a decent match. He or she can come up with valuable ideas that can bring you faster success for your program.

While a business-to-business mail order operator can manage to do his or her own compiling under certain circumstances, it's difficult to imagine a do-it-yourself effort in a *consumer* campaign. The job of compiling many thousands of individual's names from public records in order to build a list would be a nightmare and the results almost surely a disappointment.

Let's take a deeper look at how to decide whether you're better off with a proprietary or compiled list and how to start defining *exactly* what you need.

DECIDING ON THE STRONGEST POSSIBLE LIST FOR YOUR DIRECT MAIL NEEDS

If you plan on mailing to consumers, by all means obtain a *proprietary* list. Try to identify people who have made *prior direct mail purchases*. Compiled consumer lists can make sense only if you're in a position to send out enormous quantities of mailers on a regular basis. Remember this important fact:

> Retail buyers are *not* mail order buyers! A mail order purchaser has clearly demonstrated a willingness to buy something without having to first see it in the flesh, but a retail customer *does* require that contact. Therefore, if a list broker tells you that good lists of prior *retail* buyers are available, *decline* them. They simply will not produce the results you're after. Insist on previous *mail order buyers*.

If at all possible, specify a proprietary list of individuals who have purchased products or services in the same general class as what *you* are offering. To illustrate, if you are selling budget clothing items, a list of high-fashion Paris-inspired evening dress buyers probably won't do you much good. But a line of books on do-it-yourself repairs might very well sell briskly to recent buyers of older homes.

For business-to-business mailers, the situation isn't quite as obvious as it is for consumer markets. First, you aren't dealing with the same kind of crushing numbers in the business community as you would be in targeting households. A larger U.S. city could have about 10,000 business establishments, but perhaps 450,000 or more consumer names.

So, if you obtain a compiled list of the 10,000 firms, you certainly *would* get a bunch of companies that are too small, in the wrong businesses, or deficient in some other ways. But the number of "bad" listings may not be serious enough to warrant purchase of a proprietary list at much higher cost. That's a question best answered by a reputable list broker in your area.

Without question, one of the truly important features of a proprietary business list is the probable existence of *specific buyer names*. *That's* worth extra list money. Many companies simply won't bother to forward promotional mail with no recipient name or just a title that usually doesn't fit anyone in the firm.

Since a significant number of compiled company names will probably be missing basic data such as contact names, it can pay to do a round of precalling *if* the number of firms on the list isn't too big. Precalling can be done by a minimum wage person who finds out:

- If the firm is still at the same location, verify the address

- How many employees work there as a clue to size

- The name of the desired contact so your mailing can be directed to that person's attention

Usually these facts are available from the company's receptionist and are generally given without hesitation. While this approach does demand work and expense on your part, it surely does result in a squeaky clean and highly qualified business prospect list.

Next, here are vital things to find out from a list broker before you make any commitments.

QUESTIONS TO ASK LIST BROKERS BEFORE YOU MAKE A DECISION

When you are screening list brokers, searching for the one who will serve you best, review these points with them:

- Does the broker have the ability to rent you a list that embodies these basic prospect profile characteristics?

FOR CONSUMER LISTS	FOR BUSINESS LISTS
Prior mail order buyer and/or ...	Industry type
Marital status	Number of employees
Education	How many branch offices
Occupation	Location of branches
Income	Name of contact (buyer)
Family size	Complete address, phone number
Home owner or renter	
Tenure in residence	
Value, if home	
Complete address, phone number	
Carrier Route Information if you plan to mail bulk rate	

- How many names are available? This is called the *universe*. If you specify certain prospect characteristics in an attempt to zero in on the best possible group, you'll find out from the broker if the universe is the right size for your promotional needs.

- How meticulously has the list been maintained? Your broker should be able to tell you how frequently updates are made. Weekly or monthly changes should give you a high level of deliverability.

   Lists age fast. It's not at all uncommon to see *30 percent a year changes*. Thus, problems might be in store if a list is updated only every six months or less. Eighty percent accuracy/deliverability is acceptable.

- *Format* is the way the list is delivered to you, whether on computer disk, printout or some other way. More about commonly available list formats appears later in this chapter.

The following items are of fundamental importance when you rent *proprietary* lists:

- *Recency* is how long ago prospects purchased by mail order. The more recent, the better your list. Try to get a list where purchases were made within the *last 90 days*.

- *Frequency* is how often prospects purchase by mail order. You'd be in good shape if your people last bought within 90 days and typically make such purchases about every three months.

- *Value of purchase* is how much your targeted prospects spend. A list of consumers who spend $10 per purchase may not respond to a $79 offer.

Recency, frequency, and value of purchase are primarily consumer list characteristics, and don't usually apply to lists of business firms.

All brokers should be able to give you *list data cards* on proprietary lists. These cards generally include a detailed background about the list in question, thus helping you come to a decision.

Now we'll discuss list formats you can request from most brokers.

LIST FORMATS YOU CAN SPECIFY

Before describing the various list formats a broker can supply, it's important to touch briefly on the difference between a mailing list and a database.

- A mailing list contains just the information you need to get your promotion delivered. For example,

Herman Cairns, Marketing Manager
J.F. Carlson Company
644 Western Place, Suite 700
Wescott, MN 28077

- If your broker provided certain profile information that you requested when you ordered your list, you get much more data than just the basic four mailing lines shown. You received something like

NAME:	J. F. Carlson Company
ADDRESS:	644 Western Place, Suite 700
CITY:	Wescott
STATE:	MN
ZIP:	28077
PHONE:	(604) 222-0011
LOCATION:	HQ
EMPLOYEES:	55
CONTACT:	Herman Cairns
TITLE:	Marketing manager
INDUSTRY	8602

- This is a *database*. It provides *all* the information you asked your broker to provide, which may be everything the broker is *able* to provide.

We'll go a little more deeply into databases in the section on Computerizing Your Prospect Base later in this chapter. Right now, we want to explore the ways your *mailing list* can be set up by your broker so your promotion gets into the hands of buyers.

Here are the list formats you'll no doubt select from:

- *Labels* are available in these formats:

Cheshire labels are frequently used for mass mail. They are white, rectangular paper labels affixed to envelopes, packages, and publications.

State of the art is a four-up Cheshire label, whereby one page has four vertical columns of names and addresses, with 11 names per column, or a total of 44 names per page. Using special machines (called Cheshires), up to 30,000 envelopes can be addressed every hour. That includes cutting, gluing, and applying the labels to envelopes.

Pressure-sensitive labels work on the peel-and-stick principle. For smaller-scale mailings, the required manual task may be tolerable. This label generally costs a little more than Cheshires.

As a point of interest, pressure-sensitive *piggyback* labels are valuable in promotions that ask a buyer to peel off the mailing label and put it on an enclosed order form or reply card so that response device gets back to the seller.

- *Computer diskettes* are sometimes used to address mailers. A good mailing service can use the diskette you receive from your broker to print envelopes by inkjet. This produces a crisp, personal looking address.

  Some individual direct mailers can address their own envelopes if they are equipped with a decent printer, an envelope feeder, and a software program that can make it all happen.

- *Printouts* on ordinary computer paper can be used if typewriting or hand addressing is to be done on small mailings.

Before you make any major commitments on big mailing lists, make as sure as humanly possible that you're on the right track with the list you selected! That's covered next.

TESTING CHECKLIST

"If you can't measure it, *don't do it*!" More than a few mail order veterans have uttered those words. Here's a case in point that illustrates what that statement means:

In an effort to expand his customer base, Herb Bailer mails a small crafts catalog to 100,000 consumers twice a year. He sends this mailing to various compiled and proprietary lists. But before Herb commits to sending out the entire promotion, he routinely conducts three small test mailings of 5,000 each.

This entrepreneur holds off on spending his budgeted funds for 85,000 names until he has some solid evidence about which of three lists is apt to produce best and which of three offers appears strongest. Bailer estimates that the extra effort he puts out in testing has increased results by as much as 30 percent since he started in business three years ago.

Large-scale mail order operators test *everything* before they roll out massive promotions. The checklist you'll see in a moment includes most of the important components that can be evaluated. Smaller-scale mail order firms should, *at the very least*, test for the best list and the best offer, as Herb Bailer does.

A successful sampling gives you the ability to project, with reasonable precision, the results of a bigger effort later on. Bailer can't conceive of mailing to 85,000 consumers without some prior indication of what might happen.

How *extensively* to test before promotion rollout depends on several things: First, how big will your total mailing be? In the case of a consumer mailing, if you can budget a promotion to only 10,000 names, it doesn't really make much sense to conduct a couple of tests of 2,500 each, leaving a mere 5,000 rollout.

For small mail order firms, tests should involve at least 2,500 names. A sampling like that should provide a conclusive comparison.

Second, can you comfortably budget sufficient funds to develop *two or three* different promotions to test? Remember, only the best one will be rolled out and the losers discarded.

Use a copy of the following checklist every time you work out testing for a promotion. It will serve to remind you of the areas to consider. Use *only* the tests you feel are most useful.

IMPORTANT: If you decide to test only for best offer and best list, a sample mailing for *each* is needed because you can test for only *one* conclusion at a time. For example, *one* test mailing can't show you both the best list *and* the best offer since you will never be sure which factor was responsible for favorable results.

TESTING CHECKLIST

Testing for the Best Offer

In *one* of the following categories, test two or more different approaches to find out which does best:

☐ Buying incentive (two-for-one versus 50 percent discount, etc.)

Describe:

Offer 1: _____

Offer 2: _____

Offer 3: _____

Note: Be sure to file an exact sample of each offer for future reference.

☐ Product or service

Describe:

Offer 1: _____

Offer 2: _____

Offer 3: _____

☐ Mailer format (envelope mailing versus self-mailer, etc.)

Describe:

Offer 1: _____

Offer 2: _____

Offer 3: _____

☐ Enclosed promotional elements

Describe:

Offer 1:_____

Offer 2:_____

Offer 3:_____

☐ Envelope "teaser" copy

Describe:

Offer 1:_____

Offer 2:_____

Offer 3:_____

☐ Print colors (two-color versus black and white, etc.)

Describe:

Offer 1:_____

Offer 2:_____

Offer 3:_____

☐   Mailing method (first class versus bulk rate, etc.)

Describe:

Offer 1: _____

Offer 2: _____

Offer 3: _____

☐   Response method (800 number versus mail-in orders, etc.)

Describe:

Offer 1: _____

Offer 2: _____

Offer 3: _____

☐   Other

Describe:

Offer 1: _____

Offer 2: _____

Offer 3: _____

Testing for the Best List

To identify the best list, send equal-sized samplings of *one* offer to two or more different lists.

☐ Describe:

List 1: _____

Compiled_____ Proprietary_____ Population_____

List 2: _____

Compiled_____ Proprietary_____ Population_____

List 3: _____

Compiled_____ Proprietary_____ Population_____

☐ Offer used for this test: _____

☐ Date of test mailing:_____

☐ Number mailed in each sampling: _____

Notes:_____
_____
_____
_____

CODING PROMOTIONS AND LISTS SO YOU KNOW WHERE THE ACTION IS

Jenny Miranda runs identical ads in different publications almost every month. In addition, she tests mailers on various lists to find the ones that pull best. Orders come in on her 800 line, and the daily mail brings a bewildering array of different order forms. If this financial services entrepreneur didn't have a system for easily identifying the *source* of each order, she'd never be able to discern good promotions from bad or powerful lists from useless ones.

When Jenny uses the same promotion on several different lists, she goes to a little extra expense to make one tiny change to the order form that will set it apart from others. That change is one line of copy added to her address. It looks like this:

> Company Name
> Address
> City, State, Zip
> Attention: Department 301

On test lists B and C, that line reads Department 302 and Department 303, respectively. So when orders arrive from three different lists, the responsible source is instantly known.

When different promotions are tried on one list, a small change is made to the order form. That change can be a difference in design, or special department numbers, as was just described.

Call-ins are just as easy to code. Just under the toll-free 800 number, the customer is instructed in bold print to ask for a certain individual for ordering assistance. For example, in one recent case:

Sue Peterson was list number 1

Robert Phillips was list number 2

Carol Hampton was list number 3

These are strictly code names. Whoever is taking orders when a call comes in says "Sue is off today, I can help you." Extension numbers can also be used for coding, even if you have just one incoming line.

When your full-scale program is rolled out, the need for coding is no less important. Orders will trickle in for many weeks or months and will overlap newer promotions. Coding *will* prevent confusion under those circumstances.

Once you have taken measures to select good lists and prove their pulling power through testing, it's time to set up a system for *keeping* those lists in top shape. That's our next topic.

KEEPING YOUR LIST SQUEAKY CLEAN

There is no way to say too much about the importance of your *customer* and *prospect* lists. As the most valuable assets in a mail order business, they have to be meticulously kept up. List maintenance works best when one person takes the responsibility of updating them at *definite intervals*. Once every two or three months is frequent enough to keep a list sharp.

Any direct mailer who has used an outdated list can attest to the expense and aggravation that accompanies a flood of undeliverable mailers. A consumer list that hasn't been updated in a year or so can run as high as 50 percent undeliverable. Business lists don't change quite as drastically, but can still be badly off the mark if neglected.

Good list maintenance includes these steps:

- At a little extra cost, the postal service will notify you about new addresses for consumers or businesses that have moved. Instructions like the following, printed on the envelope, are required:

ADDRESS CORRECTION REQUESTED —
RETURN POSTAGE GUARANTEED

Check with the postal service to make sure about currently approved language, and where it should appear on the envelope.

- As new prospects are identified, the periodic list maintenance session is used to add these names.

  Also, new lists may be added to an existing prospect base. When this is done, a "merge/purge" operation is necessary to eliminate duplicates, which are both expensive and potentially embarrassing. Some word processing software programs for personal computers are capable of doing compares that match and purge duplicated names. Or a good mailing service can handle the task at reasonable cost.

- In business-to-business direct mail, precalling was mentioned earlier in this handbook. The receptionist in a prospect firm can verify the mailing address, identify the right buyer name, tell the caller exactly what the firm does, and provide information on the size of the company, all in a matter of a minute or so.

  It can pay to precall if you are dealing with a small business list, *and* if your product or service is high enough in value to absorb the cost of the precalling operation.

If you feel yourself getting a little down when you face the chore of updating, remember this:

Most sales are made after the *fifth attempt*. But most sellers give up after the second try. When you update your list on a regular basis—and keep hitting it with promotions—success will be yours!

A word now about protecting yourself.

KEEPING YOUR VALUABLE CUSTOMER LIST SAFE

If a competitor of yours could get his hands on your hard-earned customer list, you'd have your hands full. It would represent a monumental setback in your business career. Experts agree that these four security measures can and *should* be taken by mail order operators to prevent theft:

- *A backup copy* of your customer list should be kept at some secure location away from your office. Whether the names are on a computer disk or a printout, make sure you always have an extra set to put away. This minimizes the impact of theft and gives you the ability to continue in business without interruption in the event of damage to your office.

- *Limit access* to your customer list. The person who does the updating should be fully trusted by you and perhaps may be the *only* other individual besides you who can get at the customer list.

- If your customer list is on a personal computer in your office, try to acquire software that provides *password protection* for selected files. If that special code word isn't known by others, they can't access your customer list.

- When a broker or mailing service is to maintain your customer list, check out that firm by contacting some of its old customers. Do everything you can to make sure they're ethical.

YOUR OWN DATABASE: REACHING A NEW LEVEL OF DIRECT MARKETING POWER

Mitchell Goldklank of LCS Direct Marketing Services defines database this way:

> A database is information that qualifies the propensity of a consumer to use a specific product or service.

Most of us use a database every day when we refer to a telephone book. If each name in the phone book was scribbled on a separate piece of paper and then randomly dumped into a mountain of paper, its value would be nil. By alphabetizing names, the first step is taken toward building a database.

In our example, the value of this database is further enhanced through the creation of a classified (Yellow Pages) phone book. With it, we not only have alphabetical listings but also easy-to-find categories by business type.

A database, then, is simply a refined list, coded and segmented according to certain characteristics of the list's population. You can use a database to zero in on *certain types* of customers and prospects. Jim Herdling markets rare old photographs. He has to have the ability to select *instantly* which customers or prospects are to receive certain new additions to his line. As a case in point, Jim can select just retailers for a mailing of old department store shots, or maritime firms for seagoing pictures.

According to Joe Grosidier of PrimeNet DataSystems, list enhancement typically includes:

- Geo-code appending—or applying a census guide file to a customer list to segment the file for results analysis

- Demographic/life-style data appending—which is the addition of information gathered from different vendors on a household or business list

- Telephone number appending—or adding phone numbers to lists

- Standardization—the conversion of data into usable formats, if it currently is not

- Merge/purge operations

Once a list is enhanced and coded, it is segmented so that specific customers and prospect groups can be accessed. Your mailing list can then be extracted from this database according to the type of prospect or customer you want for a specific promotion.

You probably realize that an undertaking like this demands the services of a database management company. A good firm can sit down with you and work out a strategy that will serve you well years into the future. If successful direct marketing is an objective dear to you, you are strongly urged to take that step. The investment will pay in ways that go beyond better sales. Here's one of those ways.

RENTING YOUR LIST FOR BIG EXTRA INCOME

Some mail order operators are dead-set against renting out their customer lists, regardless of the big income they stand to rake in. One very successful company has built a roster of 28,000 active buyers. Scores of noncompetitive companies would jump at the chance to pay $100 per thousand, or more, to do one mailing to this list. But the founder steadfastly refuses even to consider the $2,800 per deal windfall, preferring instead to keep his customers a secret.

To rent or not is a decision that is strictly up to you. When you have succeeded in building a list of at least 3,000 customers, you *will* have the opportunity to make extra money on those names. While many list brokers want a minimum of 5,000 consumer names, the smaller number should attract some renters. Business lists can be smaller, but still be very attractive. One financial consultant rents a ist of only 1,200 trade associations for $350. Rental arrangements usually work this way:

- A customer list that qualifies in terms of recency, frequency, and order size should command $100 per thousand names. That entitles the renter to *one* mailing, unless some other arrangement is agreed on.

- Your broker generally takes a 20 percent commission, or $20 per thousand. The broker also charges about $10 to $20 per thousand initially to set the list up so it can be rented to others. Then the list is maintained by the broker, a nice bonus for the renter.

As the owner of a list for rent, you can and *should* impose some restrictions such as no phone calls to your customers, no rentals to direct competitors, and conformance to certain ethical and quality standards in the renter's offer. Your broker should contact you for an okay to rent before going ahead.

To give yourself an extra measure of security, it's a good idea to seed your list with a few decoys to make sure renters observe established limitations. For example, include the names of some friends and relatives in your list and ask them to let you know what kind of contacts they receive from renters. Most brokers will also use decoys of their own.

List swaps between competitors and noncompetitors alike are gaining in popularity, especially in the trading of older lists. Two firms that have similar customer counts can *both* benefit under these circumstances: a couple of companies that offer basically the same products or services to their customers in mailing after mailing will inevitably run into declining results. But a *fresh* offer to those tired lists can dramatically increase response, so both marketers stand to win.

Remember, when you rent your list to another firm, people they sell become fair game. Essentially, you'll be sharing those buyers with the renting firm. But when you rent to noncompetitive organizations, that should not have much impact on you.

What should your direct mail piece look like? The next chapter is devoted to answering that important question.

CHAPTER 8

AD AND MAILER FORMATS THAT COMMAND THE ATTENTION OF BUYERS

Simple is effective. You *don't* need complex, costly promotion designs to grab the eye of mail order buyers. Busy shoppers welcome clear, direct messages. They want to get *right to the point* without unfolding flap after flap and reading long paragraphs of copy. An ad or mailer has to grasp a prospect's attention in *a few seconds*. A shopper will dig into the details of your offer *only* if his or her interest has been sparked at first glance.

To reinforce that point, Bill Jayme, one of America's top promotional writers, and Heikki Ratalakti, a renowned designer who works with Jayme, question whether elaborate devices like "yes," "no," and "maybe" stickers, or jumbo envelopes and the like, pull better. The two experts say it's whatever makes the offer interesting that really counts.

This chapter describes straightforward ad designs and direct mail approaches that have achieved excellent results year after year. They work for both consumer and business promotions. While you *can* spend lots more money to create elaborate ads and mailers, the extra costs and margin for error don't pay off for small beginning operations.

You'll also discover which components of a promotion are most important in doing the selling job and how those elements should be set up to give you the best possible response.

SETTING UP YOUR PROMOTIONS PROFESSIONALLY
AND ECONOMICALLY

If you are not an experienced ad writer, you should seriously consider enlisting the aid of a person who is. Your ad or direct mail package doesn't have to be an award winner, but it definitely must look crisp and professional.

U.S. population centers are full of free-lancers who are delighted to work with you at reasonable rates on two important areas:

1. *Developing headlines and descriptive copy.* In addition, you may want help in working out text for cover letters, order forms, guarantees, and other components.

2. *Assisting with the production of ads or mailers.* This includes a layout of the promotion and then creation of the camera-ready boards used by the printer. This graphics phase also includes selection of type, processing of photos or illustrations, and other steps required to produce the finished promotional piece. When you are able to provide strong guidance to a free-lancer, costs go down and results are better. So it pays to get your ideas firmly set *before* you sit down with an outside support person.

You may be able to find one reasonably priced free-lancer who can do both copywriting *and* graphics, or a small shop that employs people skilled in both specialties. Advertising agencies are *not* a good choice since their rates are usually geared to larger programs and heavy media purchases.

If you choose to take on the task of doing the creative work yourself, *at least* have the copy edited before it's printed. A sharp journalism major might be able to handle that. When undertaking a copy development project, see what the manufacturer of your mail order product or service has available. Also check on competitive ads for ideas. A printer can often help you with all production procedures at extra cost if you want to avoid that task.

Most important, *whoever* helps you out with development, the printed piece *has to convey the feeling you want..* So you have to be especially vigilant at *every step*—from rough drafts and sketches to camera-ready boards. You can always make changes *before* the job is printed.

If possible, talk to five or six free-lancers. Ask to see what kind of work they have produced for other clients and how much they charge. Since you won't really know how much work has to go into your promotion, get *flat rate* fees instead of hourly rates. The shop you select should give you a list of the steps they agree to perform so no conflicts arise later.

The more you know about mailing formats and components, the better you'll be at giving guidance to free-lancers. This chapter provides the information you need to get top performance.

We'll begin with the how-to's of creating simple but effective media ads.

WHAT MAKES MEDIA ADS WORK

Put yourself in the shoes of a magazine or newspaper reader who is open to purchasing by mail. A combination of elements captures your interest.

David Morgan's mail order ad for a Celtic Cross pendant, shown in Figure 8-1, utilizes two devices to attract shoppers: (1) a photograph that clearly shows the extraordinary design of the piece and (2) the

Figure 8-1. A Small Ad That Gets the Message Across

headline in Celtic, *Croes Geltaidd*, that practically demands the further attention of jewelry buyers with an eye for the exotic. This ad packs heavy punch into a small space.

Limited space is the ever-present challenge to mail order ad designers. A concise message spearheaded by a brief power-packed headline and a compelling photo or illustration are the keys to hard-hitting mail order ads. The smaller the space, the more resourceful the designer has to be.

In conceiving the ad, your first objective is to conjure up a picture of *who the prospect will be*. Then an appeal is created to reach that specific target.

Ad creators knew from magazine demographic data that readers of this particular publication are affluent and older, a category very likely to spend money on unusual jewelry or on gifts for loved ones.

Testimonials are great convincers. Even a one-sentence statement can add tremendous credibility to a small ad. Praise from a satisfied user is apt to be believed by a prospect who might be skeptical about self-promotion from the seller.

Some media advertisers believe that mail order ads can be simple for this reason: many readers already want what you're selling. They are "in the market" and simply searching for a good source. A direct headline, appealing illustration, and reasonable price will be sufficient to trigger the purchase. Based on that line of reasoning, you probably will *not* sell a reader who is not already presold to some extent.

Media advertisers have to conform precisely to publication mechanical requirements. The magazine or newspaper has to receive your ad in *exactly* the correct size and in a form prescribed by the publication. Figure 8-2 shows one magazine's mechanical requirements.

Almost any graphic designer should be equipped to handle the production of your ad so it meets specifications like these.

Now we'll move on to mailer formats, and see how they can be set up to get great results.

Figure 8-2. Ad Mechanical Requirements Provided by a Publication

MECHANICAL REQUIREMENTS

Non-Bleed sizes	Two-page spread	15 x 9-7/8"
	Full page	7 x 9-7/8"
	2/3 page	9-7/8 x 4-5/16"
	1/2 page (vert.)	3-7/16 x 9-7/8"
	1/2 page (horiz.)	7 x 4-7/8"
	1/3 page (vert.)	2-1/4 x 9-7/8"
	1/3 page (horiz.)	4-5/8 x 4-7/8"
	1/6 page (vert.)	2-14 X 4-7/8"
Bleed sizes	Two-page spread	16-1/4 x 11-1/8"
	Full page	8-1/4 x 11-1/8"

Live matter within 7-1/8 x 10-1/8". Allow 1/8" trim—
top, bottom and side trimmed. Keep live matter 1/4" from gutter
and 3/8" from trimmed sides.

PRINTING SPECIFICATIONS

Printed—Web offset   Binding—Saddle stitched
Screens—Black & white or two-color: 110-120 line screen. Four-
color: 120-133 line screen

Total screen density on all flat tints and solids 240%. No more
than one solid color.

The following materials are acceptable for reproduction:
    4-color-film negatives emulsion up
    B&W or 2-color-film negatives or black-and-white
    reproduction proofs.
Submit two sets of progressive proofs on 80# white enamel using
standard process color or match print.

Center marks requested. If proofs are not supplied, quality of
reproduction and registration is at the risk of the advertiser.
Additional charge at cost will be made for separation or
modification of artwork, film, etc. All separations and/or B&W film
and stripping charges will be invoiced to advertiser at cost.

A DESCRIPTION OF "THE MAGIC SIX" MAILING PACKAGE COMPONENTS

There are three basic types of direct mail packages:

1. *A "classic" package.* This consists of an envelope that holds five separate pieces, all of which help to make the sale. This outer envelope, plus the five inserts inside of it, constitute the Magic Six mailing components.

2. *A self-mailer* that incorporates on a single sheet of paper each of the same elements found in the classic package.

3. *A catalog* used to present a wider selection of goods and/or services. A catalog should also be designed to include each of the Magic Six components.

Without doubt, you receive a staggering array of direct mail formats every week, and each one looks unique in its own way. But virtually every one is based strictly on the Magic Six principle. As a starting direct mail operator, sticking with this *proven method* is the way to go. Here are the basics on what each of the Magic Six components do:

- *The mailing envelope* simply holds all the other components, but can and *should* go considerably further than that by carrying copy that urges the prospect to open it and read the contents.

- *The order form or reply device* is the means by which your prospect responds to your offer, whether by purchasing or requesting more information, as the case may be.

  It is interesting that surveys indicate many mail recipients go to the order form *first* because it always capsulizes the essence of the offer. Due to that major role, a response device *has to sell effectively!*

- *The product/service brochure* is devoted to describing the offer. It can be anything from a simple black and white letter-size sheet up to a huge full-color foldout. However it's designed, the brochure is generally the most graphic element of the Magic Six.

- *The cover letter* is intended to give your mailing package a strong personalized feeling. Rather than repeating product or service attributes already covered in the brochure, this letter helps build trust and credibility in the prospect.

- *The gift insert* carries the free item offer, if one is to be included in your program. There is strong proof that when the buying inducement is presented on *a small separate piece,* it attracts more consumer attention.

   Some mail promoters claim good results by putting their guarantee terms on a separate insert instead of in the brochure or cover letter.

- *The reply envelope* does its share of selling by making response easier for the buyer. Ideally, this envelope is preaddressed and postage paid.

Each of these components is explored more fully in this chapter. We'll start right now.

WHAT COMPELS BUYERS TO OPEN YOUR ENVELOPE? TIPS FROM TOP EXPERTS

An effective message, possibly combined with eye-catching graphics, can turn an ordinary outer envelope into a formidable direct mail selling device. Postal Service regulations give you the opportunity to use a substantial portion of the envelope front, and almost all the back, for your own promotional purposes (check with your local Postal Service branch for the most current regulations).

Pat Crutchfield of Westvaco, a major envelope supplier based in Springfield, Massachusetts, described the vast array of special treatments available for direct mail envelopes:

- *"Jumbo" specialty envelopes* are large, side-seam envelopes that provide maximum surface area for multicolor graphics.

- *Special windows* allow "sneak previews" of specially designed mailer contents. Windows can be created in a variety of shapes and placed to arouse interest.

- *Action mailers* are especially effective in direct mail. They can be designed to open by lifting a tab, tearing a perforation, scratching a hidden symbol, removing a label, or other means that involve the recipient.

- *Holograms* create totally unique graphics effects. A hologram is a colorful, three-dimensional image that gives an envelope dramatic impact.

"The primary role of the envelope in any direct mail promotion is to be creative enough to entice and attract attention . . . involve the recipients and arouse curiosity . . . stimulate them to pick up the envelope, open it, and read the contents."

Figure 8-3 shows the front of a 6-inch by 9-inch outer envelope used by a publisher to arouse the interest of prospects.

Figure 8-3. An Outer Envelope That Begs to Be Opened

It's bold and practically screams for the attention of the recipient. Another great envelope format looks like this:

> The Reader's Digest Sweepstakes mailer is a classic. One envelope used measured 6 inches by 11 inches and had *three* different windows. One gave the recipient a peek inside at a real metal key to a new car that could be won. Another window revealed two gold-tone seals that " . . . could be worth $125,000.00 to you . . . " The third showed the addressee, and
>
> MISS LEE WEBB
> WILL BE THE WINNER OF
> $5,000,000.00

This is an exceedingly difficult promotion to ignore. It's loaded with visual interest and promises of enormous wealth.

While you may not be ready at this time to undertake an envelope of such spectacular expense and design in your direct mail program, the example serves the purpose of pointing out the possibilities open to you. Make sure that your designer fully understands the capabilities of top envelope makers. They are, for the most part, delighted to work with you to create outer envelopes that will help rivet the attention of your prospects.

The next Magic Six mailing package component we'll look at is the reply device.

HOW YOUR ORDER FORM CAN BECOME
A POWERFUL CLOSER

First, let's again define the difference between an order form and a reply device:

- An order form is used in any promotion that is intended to make an immediate sale. The form enables a buyer to specify selections, calculate the payment due, and provide a correct delivery address. In almost every case, an order form has to be enclosed in a reply envelope by the purchaser. That envelope is one of the Magic Six mail package components, covered a bit later.

Figure 8-4 illustrates an order form.

Figure 8-4. An Outstanding Order Form. It's Big, Well-Designed and Easy-To-Use

1. ORDERED BY (please print)	2. GIFT ORDER OR SHIP TO: (use only if different than ordered by)
Name _____	☐ Mr. ☐ Mrs. ☐ Ms.
Street _____ Apt. # _____	Name _____
City _____ State ____ Zip ____	Street _____ Apt. # _____
Day Phone ( ) _____	City _____ State ____ Zip ____
Evening Phone ( ) _____	Gift Message (40-character limit)

3. PAYMENT METHOD

Please, no currency

☐ Check or Money Order — amount enclosed $ _____
(Please make checks or money orders payable to Best Products Co., Inc.)

☐ MasterCard
☐ VISA   ☐ DISCOVER

Expiration Date Required: Month [ ]   Year [ ]
Complete Card Number: [ ][ ][ ][ ][ ][ ][ ][ ][ ][ ]

MasterCard Interbank No. [ ][ ][ ]

Customer Signature _____   Date _____

4. ITEMS

Catalog Number	Description (Specify Color or Personalization)	Size	Qty.	Price Each	Shipping Weight (×) Qty.	Total Price Price Each (×) Qty.

(If more space is needed, use a separate sheet of paper.)

TELEPHONE ORDERS ACCEPTED DAILY
8AM - MIDNIGHT EASTERN TIME

SALES TAX
To avoid delays in filling and shipping your order, please see page 403K for listing of states where sales tax must be paid.

Total Weight	Zone Rate Per Pound	Shipping Charge
	×	=

We are a member of the Direct Marketing Association.

Total Freight Weight	
Total Merchandise	
Sales Tax	
Shipping Charge (see minimums)	
Handling Charge	1.95
Other Fees	
Grand Total	

Thank You For Your Order

(Cut along dotted line)

- A reply device is usually a request for additional information, used in promotions intended to generate leads. It simply offers the prospect a *Yes! Send me more information* box to check or perhaps a yes/no option, as discussed earlier. Since not much space is required for that additional information request, reply devices can be postcard size and printed on stock heavy enough to be self-mailed. The reverse side is set up in a business reply format.

Both the request side and mailing side of a reply card are shown in Figure 8-5.

Many direct mail recipients initially reach for the order form or reply device since it neatly summarizes the offer. It tells the prospect exactly what action is required and how much money is involved. By virtue of that fact, *don't forget* to recap the offer as concisely as possible. For example,

> Yes! Rush me your 30-day, total vitamin program.
> $14.95 is enclosed.

Then, once an interested shopper knows what's involved, he or she will go back and review your brochure, cover letter, satisfaction guarantee, and other mailing package components.

Diane Ruby oversees a highly successful mailing program for an international skin care company. She makes these observations about order forms and reply cards:

> "A formula we've been using has improved response about 10 percent. We make our order form look official with banknote borders and lots of type. It's big and has the look of a valuable document, so prospects take it more seriously. We actually call it a request form, not an order form."

Other important tips are:

- When you use a *separate sheet* for your order form or reply device, it will do better than if it's part of some other component.

- If possible, repeat a picture of your free gift on the order form. Also, consider attaching a receipt stub that the prospect can remove and keep.

Product and service brochures are reviewed next.

Figure 8-5. Reply Card

Front   **Back**

To upgrade to HBO®/Cinemax® at special
subscriber savings, call now or use the
Instant Work Order below!

GET INSTALLATION OF HBO
OR HBO AND CINEMAX
AT TERRIFIC SAVINGS!
SEE OTHER SIDE FOR DETAILS

HBO/CINEMAX
INSTANT WORK ORDER

☐ *YES!* I want to order HBO and Cinemax and have
them installed at terrific savings.*

☐ *YES!* I want to order HBO and have it installed
at terrific savings.*

☐ **Maybe.** I still have a few questions. Please call me
with details. I understand I am under no obligation.

NAME_____
                     (Please Print)
ADDRESS_____

CITY_____ STATE_____ ZIP_____

PHONE_____ BEST TIME TO CALL_____

Mail this card or call today!

*Monthly Cable TV and HBO/Cinemax fees are additional. Offer available only to new HBO/Cinemax
subscribers. HBO/Cinemax may not be substituted for any other premium services. Cinemax service
may not be available in all areas. Offer may apply to standard installation on one TV set in wired
serviceable areas. Offer may vary. Other restrictions may apply. Call your local cable company for
complete offer details.
S

DON'T WAIT!

Installation of HBO or HBO and
Cinemax for Only $5.00*

Big Entertainment That Never Stops!

Call Now for Details! Offer Expires 10/5/90
TCI CABLEVISION

527-7545
in North Seattle

S803222   Local taxes may apply. Please call for details.

PLACE
STAMP
HERE

TCI CABLEVISION
1140 NORTH 94 STREET
SEATTLE WA 98103

S803222

BUILDING SALES POWER INTO YOUR PRODUCT OR SERVICE BROCHURE

A brochure is, very simply, the device used to sell your product or service. Your choice of a product brochure format is mostly a function of how many items you want to present to prospects. For example,

A few items or less can be effectively presented on a single sheet.

Such a simple circular can produce phenomenal results. Art Edels sells unusual musical instruments by mail. He uses an oversized foldout circular that shows *one* product in dramatic proportions. This approach does strong business consistently.

A dozen or so items may require two pages, such as an 11-inch by 17-inch sheet folded into a two-pager.

When the product array gets up in quantity, a bound catalog might be the answer.

If the catalog is rather small, say, 8 to 16 pages, the other Magic Six mailing package components can be kept separate. In larger books, you should consider making those other components part of the catalog itself.

Regardless of *which* format you decide on, it should include certain elements that will help make it an effective seller. Those elements are:

- If possible, an *overall* headline that captures the theme of your entire product or service line. For example,

   Hard-to-find toys and games for grown-ups

- A headline for each product or service in your line.

- Descriptive copy, and a photo or illustration, for each item. Copy should emphasize not only what the product or service does, but also its price and how your offer works.

Other vital points to consider in putting together your brochure pertain to mechanical aspects:

- Can the brochure be economically produced? Use *stand-ard sizes* to help control production costs and avoid custom die-cutting and folding. Use color printing *only* if it's absolutely necessary. Designers may get carried away with radical approaches that could run costs up. Stay in close touch with your printer in order to catch needless expenses.

• Make sure the color, weight, and quality of the paper for your brochure matches the other components in your package.

Consider our next Magic Six component: the cover letter.

FIVE WAYS TO MAKE COVER LETTERS SELL HARDER

A large number of direct mail experts put the importance of a letter ahead of the reply device. It's the one package component that can very effectively personalize your offer—for the simple reason that people expect letters to be personal.

Do direct mail shoppers actually read letters? The answer is an unqualified *yes*. In fact, the best direct mail letters run two pages in length. And some very good ones can run *four* pages. Once interest is captured, prospects *will dig in* for more facts.

In truth, most direct response experts insist that the letter should *always* be long. Each additional page boosts the response rate by as much as half a percentage point, according to Frank H. Johnson, a highly respected direct marketing pioneer.

Johnson developed the concept of putting text *above* the salutation, separated from the text by a ring of asterisks. That so-called "Johnson box" effectively declares that an offer is being made. It's an eye-grabber, no question about it.

Many top writers, Johnson included, believe in sprinkling their promotional letter text with impact words like "free," "death," and "sex." They are definitely eye-stoppers!

Figure 8-6 is a direct mail letter that has been extremely effective for a highly successful marketer. Please notice, it does not include some of the characteristics just discussed, but it has been tremendously successful. Also, it doesn't get into details about products or services, but it *does* work hard on establishing rapport.

Figure 8-6—A Successful Sales Letter

****

Not one, but TWO *VALUABLE* FREE GIFTS if you act NOW!

****

Dear Friend:

Ann Delker just wrote to me—and that reminded me to send you our new catalog.

You're probably wondering why a letter from a person you don't know would remind me to mail you the Jefferson catalog, right? Here's why: You and Ann are alike in two important ways. Both of you work hard at staying in shape, and neither of you are much for the same old selection in retail stores. Ann wrote—

"When I got your catalog, I didn't really believe your sports supplies could be as good as you claimed they were. But as long as you offered complete satisfaction, I just had to find out. So I ordered cross-training shoes and a warmup outfit.

"Just as you promised, **everything was perfect—exactly what I wanted**! I thank you. Your catalog has opened up a whole new world of sports equipment for me and my family."

But that only tells *part* of the story. Here's what you can look forward to as a Jefferson customer:

- You'll get BULLETINS ON SPECIAL PURCHASES from top manufacturers. Fantastic savings are passed *directly to you*.

- On EACH AND EVERY PURCHASE YOU MAKE you'll get Jefferson's famous *No-Risk Guarantee*. You have to be completely satisfied, *in every way*.

- You'll have ONE DEPENDABLE SOURCE for EVERY sports need. Not only top equipment, but how-to books, sports travel packages and *more*!

Continued

I think I've covered everything . . . but in case I forgot something, *please call or write me*. I know Jefferson's can be as important to you as it is to Ann and so many others who care about their sports dollar.

If we receive your first order by August 20, we'll enclose a FREE CALORIE COUNTER with your delivery!

Sincerely,

Stan Jefferson

P.S. As a special get-acquainted offer, we've enclosed AN *EXTRA* BONUS certificate for you. *No purchase necessary* . . . just send it to me and receive a free gift by return mail!

* * * *

This example incorporates the five proven tactics for effective direct mail letters. Those tactics are:

- A *lead-in* that grabs the prospect's interest *"Ann Delker wrote to me and reminded me to send you our new catalog."* This DOES arouse the curiosity of most readers.

- *Benefits* spelled out in the bullets. Readers are told exactly what they will receive as Jefferson customers.

- A *guarantee*. One should appear in the letter, even if it repeats a guarantee that appears elsewhere in your promotional package.

- Action *now*. Offer a free calorie counter if an order is submitted by August 20. Or send a message like YOU MUST DO IT *NOW*. ONLY SO MANY COPIES ARE PRINTED, NO MORE.

- The *P.S.*, considered by some to be the most prominent part of any letter. This offers an extra gift, no purchase necessary. It's one more incentive to get at least some kind of action.

In designing a powerful letter, several graphic strategies help make it hit harder. Use *underlines* and *caps* to emphasize key statements. Consider a *second color*, like red in addition to black, to dramatize certain sentences or words. The more sparingly this second color is used, the more it will pop out at the reader. *Indent* and use *bullets,* as in the sample letter, to hold a prospect's attention. Finally, use *handwritten comments* to add yet more visual impact.

Since your letter can be changed with comparatively little fuss and cost, you can create different versions for different markets. As a case in point, if you mail to some new prospects along with old customers, you definitely would want a different letter for each group.

Now, our final Magic Six component.

INSERTS: A TERRIFIC APPROACH FOR CERTAIN OFFERS

Direct mail packages that hold inserts are more interesting to prospects. People tend to *read* separate inserts more readily than information printed on some larger piece. Inserts can take the form of:

- Free gift certificates

- Discount certificates

- Customer satisfaction guarantees

- New product or service introductions (these are ride-alongs, discussed earlier)

- Even testimonials have been successfully presented on separate inserts.

As Figure 8-7 illustrates, inserts can be printed in almost any shape as long as they fit into the mailing envelope. In most cases they are not designed to be returned with a consumer's order, unless a direct mail firm decides to require receipt of a free gift certificate in order to honor the gift offer.

There really are no limits to how many inserts can be packed into one envelope. One practical consideration is postage cost, which might be driven up by extra weight.

From a design standpoint, inserts should integrate with the other Magic Six components. Paper characteristics and typefaces should not clash with other package contents. At the same time, inserts *do* have to command attention.

One insert that proved to be a major winner is discussed now.

Figure 8-7. An Insert Designed to Get Immediate Response

You could be the winner
of this fabulous extra
Early Entry Prize—
a Lexus LS 400—
if you act quickly!

Dear Cardmember:

Imagine yourself behind the wheel of this unique luxury
sedan that handles like a sports car!

Fully equipped for comfort, style and performance with
rich leather upholstery, CD player, traction control,
4.0-liter V8 engine, plus powerful drive train and outstanding
fuel efficiency, the Lexus LS400 is <u>the ultimate dream machine</u>!

> Make sure you qualify for this EXTRA prize
> drawing by mailing your Entry Certificate
> <u>before the deadline</u>!

That's right. You can win this sensational new Lexus LS400
IN ADDITION TO ANY OF THE CASH PRIZES you may have already won!

Some lucky Cardmember is GUARANTEED to win this exciting
new car. Why shouldn't it be you!

Mail your entry today!

Sincerely,

Thomas O. Ryder

Thomas O. Ryder

*P.S. Beat the deadline for a Lexus LS400--
OR take $35,000.00 IN CASH!*

WHY GUARANTEES HELP ASSURE MAIL ORDER SUCCESS

Smoke Signal, a West Coast computer maker, found a way to get its quality story across to its dealers and their system buyers. Since each system that rolled off the assembly line was routinely subjected to exhaustive tests, the phrase "endurance certified" emerged as the best way to describe the quality control process. Figure 8-8 shows the certificate replica enclosed via insert in each direct mail package. A larger version was packed with each new computer.

Figure 8-8. The "Endurance–Certified" Tag That Builds Buyer Confidence

Guarantees for direct mail buyers are tremendously important. New prospects have no idea about your integrity as a source. In truth, many people are dubious about companies they've never heard of before. So any assurances you can provide *will help break down the resistance.* Any or all of these points can be stressed in your guarantee:

- Satisfaction is *assured*. A full, prompt, unconditional money-back guarantee is yours.

- Extensive quality-control measures are taken before orders are shipped.

- Products are completely backed up by manufacturers.

Federal regulations mandate cancellation rights for *all* mail order purchases. A customer needs no reason to return items in good condition for a refund. So your assurance of satisfaction or money back is merely a statement of action you'd have to take in any event.

A guarantee offered via insert should stand out more prominently than one tucked into a corner of your product brochure. It will be even more visible if it has ornate, certificate-type borders. Guarantee inserts will look especially valuable if printed on banknote paper, which any printer should be able to obtain.

In addition to creating an insert for your guarantee, your satisfaction assurance *should* at least be mentioned in your letter and possibly in your brochure as well.

Here is one further word on just how much to send prospects.

HOW "INFO-JAMMING" BUILDS BUYER EXCITEMENT AND CREDIBILITY

Lots of copy and many mailer components suggest you have plenty to say. And if you have plenty to say, you usually appear to be good at what you do and enthusiastic about your business. Busy packages *are* fun for people to thumb through, particularly for those shoppers who are inclined to purchase by mail.

While you may stick to the Magic Six direct mail components, there are really no limitations on *how many* brochures you enclose or *how many* inserts you include.

A sparse package is in danger of looking and feeling weak—unless its job is to sell a $75,000 solid gold necklace, which might need a simple but elegant presentation.

An excellent example of info-jamming is illustrated in Figure 8-9.

This package has no fewer than *nine components!* It's used by a firm that sells a business opportunity program. Prospects buy both how-to materials and products for resale. Here's a description of each piece in this remarkably effective broadside:

1. Window mailing (outer) envelope.

2. Membership application (order form). This piece includes the prospect's address which shows through the window in the mailing envelope.

**Figure 8-9. A Great Info-Jamming Example:
9 Components in a Mailing Package**

3. Four-page letter.

4. Twenty-four-page booklet describing the business and merchandise available to members.

5. Fourteen-page booklet devoted to testimonials.

6. Eight-page newsletter with features about success stories and merchandise trends.

7. Insert 1: One-page piece showing potential member income.

8. Insert 2: Membership discount offer certificate.

9. Business reply envelope.

For a prospect who is even marginally interested in this deal, the impact can be tremendous. Proof of potential success seems overwhelming by virtue of the tremendously detailed copy, abundance of photos and illustrations, and sheer number of testimonials.

This particular approach is not by any means slick or attractive. It comes across as well researched, sincere, and extremely upbeat—a perfect position for this firm's typical prospect who is searching for a viable career.

Now we'll look at the other extreme in direct mail.

SAVE GOBS OF CASH BY USING SELF-MAILERS

From an envelope stuffed with all kinds of components, we turn to the self-mailer where the key elements are printed on one sheet of paper. Self-mailers can be small, single unfolded pieces, or works that are folded with exquisite complexity, and open up to fabulous table-top size.

As you would imagine, self-mailer production costs are generally lower than envelope mailing packages since the entire job can be completed in one printing and no inserting is needed. In addition, a self-mailer truly tests one's design skills, but there is only one piece to figure out instead of six or more.

Self-mailers can effectively include most of the vital Magic Six components. For example,

- A *reply device* is definitely included and is often perforated for easy consumer removal.

- In more elaborate self-mailers, a *business reply envelope* can be part of the single sheet. It is simply folded up by the consumer and sealed by means of adhesive edges and then used to hold the reply device or order form, as the case may be.

- A *letter* can easily be part of the design, as can the *brochure*. Some punch may be lost since the information normally conveyed by *inserts* are instead printed in the body of a self-mailer. Still, inserts *are* occasionally kept separate in self-mailers if they can be designed to stay in place during the rigors of mailing.

Some folded self-mailers are sealed by means of a small adhesive patch or are stapled. Many others are mailed unsealed.

There are a few disadvantages to self-mailers that offset their much lower cost. First, they are decidedly less personal than envelope mailings. The letter simply does not have the same feeling as a note on a separate sheet. Also, self-mailers tend to be perceived by many consumers as "junk mail" regardless of how nicely a piece is executed. Finally, you are urged to check carefully on the weight of stock you use. It has to be heavy enough to mail according to Postal Service regulations.

Experts claim that certain products and services are especially well-served by self-mailers. They are:

- Seminars and event publicity
- Offers for single products
- Promotions by retailers
- Lead-generation programs

If you are contending with a limited budget and a small product or service selection, self-mailers may very well be the way to go, whether you sell to consumers *or* businesses.

Next we discuss two of today's fastest-growing direct mail formats, newsletters and catalogs.

USING NEWSLETTERS TO SELL PRODUCTS AND SERVICES

A newsletter can carry a fascinating variety of articles that sell, inform, entertain, and powerfully build the image of a company. It can take the form of a letter-size piece printed on fine stock or an oversized tabloid on newsprint paper. Length is dictated strictly by how much you have to say—and how much your market is willing to read.

This direct mail format has just recently come into its own as a major league seller of goods and services. One of the best newsletters around is put out by a manufacturer who mails it to both prospects and customers on a bimonthly basis. The contents of one sample issue included:

- News about a trip to Hawaii offered by the firm in a customer drawing and won by a manager in a client firm.

- A new product announcement, complete with request form so readers can send for additional information.

- One personal profile about a client's employee, along with a photograph of that person.

- One profile on an employee who works for the firm that publishes the newsletter.

- Two "tech-tips" (articles that deal with user reports and applications on the firm's products). These how-to features sell lots of products.

- A puzzle, the answer to which is printed in the next issue. In addition, there is a list of those who solved the last one successfully.

- A "Where Are You?" article. Client executives who have taken jobs with unknown companies are urged to contact the firm. Lots of them are located, and they become buyers once again.

This *is* interesting reading for people in the industry. The one or two features oriented to selling products or generating leads draw as well as direct mail packages focused strictly on selling. But the newsletter has the distinct advantage of being much more friendly and low key. As such, it is read more often than mail that sells.

Newsletters make very good self-mailers. Even if you send out conventional promotional packages, a periodic newsletter may still be a strong strategy.

Next, we consider more about catalogs.

WHEN CATALOG MAILINGS PACK THE MOST PUNCH

Direct mail through thick catalogs is *not* recommended for beginning operators with small budgets. This is a format you best *grow into* over a period of time, ideally by means of a two-step program that works this way:

Through media ads, conventional direct mail, and perhaps
broadcast advertising, a substantial customer list is established.
During that process, an extensive product line is put together.
When those two aspects are well developed, the time has come
to consider catalog sales.

Setting up an effective catalog demands lots of skill and knowledge
about your market. Those skills come only through experience. Creating a costly book that isn't based on solid facts can indeed be risky.

It is also worth mentioning stock catalogs—books that are preprinted by a manufacturer, importer, or jobber and imprinted with
your company name. They *are* reasonably inexpensive, but don't do
nearly as well as "home-grown" catalogs.

Here's the bright spot: Smaller catalogs that deal with special
prospect interests most certainly can work for newer direct mail
companies. Special interests can include upscale fashion catalogs and
books that deal with *one* specialty area, such as aviation or mountain
climbing, or similar narrowly defined niches. If you can assemble a
complete product or service line that is *devoted* to such a specialty,
the next step is to obtain a list of *proven enthusiasts*. Once that is done,
you have positioned yourself for success. The final step is to create a
catalog that will captivate prospects.

In Bob Stone's excellent book, *Successful Direct Marketing
Methods* published by Crain Publishing Company in 1975, the author
describes the attributes that make a catalog a winner:

- Your visual presentation is the key to success. Unless
  you're an accomplished designer, get the help of somebody who has experience in catalog layout.

- You can't depend on the photos sometimes supplied by
  manufacturers. When shots from many different sources
  are brought together, they probably *won't* be consistent in
  style or scale. The result can be a confusing mess.

- Bigger catalogs have proven "hot spots," certain locations
  in the book that sell better than others. These are: front
  cover; inside front cover; pages 3, 4 and 5; center spread;
  the page facing the order form; inside back cover; and
  back cover.

- While the front cover *can* sell lots of items, it is often used to establish a theme for the entire catalog.

- Catalogs are powerful sellers largely because they are often retained by consumers for future reference. A thin book may be seen as a "flyer" by consumers and discarded. So catalog size *is* a positive attribute.

- Catalogs that will be sent to business firms should be standard letter size so they'll fit into files.

- Catalogs that present a number of different product or service categories do better if those categories are grouped.

Volumes have been written about direct marketing by catalog. When you get ready to embark in this challenging, profitable, but high-risk area, be sure to *research thoroughly*. The rewards can be staggering:

> Some U.S. catalog merchandisers are doing an estimated $40 million or more in annual sales, and have nearly 5 million customers.

A large catalog is definitely a format you should plan on down the road. A small specialty book is a program you may want to enter much more rapidly.

Our next chapter deals with the strongest sales maker in the field of direct marketing: *repeated contacts* with good customers and prospects.

CHAPTER 9

HOW FOLLOW-UPS MAKE BIG MONEY

Follow-up is *absolutely essential* in selling by mail order! There can be *no* substantial success without an organized approach for reselling customers and recontacting prospects who did not respond the first time you presented your offer to them.

"One-shot" promotions quite often can be a waste of your time and money. While almost any first-time promotion will succeed in attracting *some* orders, the real profits are generated when prospects start to *recognize* your offers. Immediate response is terrific, but is only the tip of the iceberg.

This chapter explains which mail order programs benefit most by using follow-up and how to use mail, telephone, and other effective methods to make follow-up work.

WHEN FOLLOW-UP WORKS BEST

In a media advertising program, you obviously can't select specific magazine or newspaper readers to see your offer a second time. You are at the mercy of the fates as to who will review your ad again. Still, media ads *definitely do better after repeated runs.* A gift advertiser said;

> "After our third run of the same ad in a new magazine, we finally begin to hit the sales pace we need to make money. Based on that information, a one- or two-time run would never work for us."

Prospect follow-up in media or broadcast advertising is actually *repeated exposure*.

In direct mail follow-up, this tricky aspect has to be solved: If you rent mailing lists, and your agreement with a broker limits you to a one-time promotion, you obviously will *not* be able to follow-up on nonbuyers. Therefore, it would be good business to negotiate an arrangement where you'd be able to send *several* mailings to the same list. Here's why that would pay:

> "Our experience shows we peak at the third mailing to the same list. In other words, we get about 75 percent of all the business there is to get after the third drop. After that, results fall so drastically it doesn't pay to stay with the same list any longer" explains the general manager of a company selling collector art objects by mail.

What about following up on *buyers*? That, of course, is where the big money is, according to the marketing director of a mail order electronics company:

> "As soon as we get an order as a result of a media ad or mailing, we intensify our efforts to sell that consumer something again. They *are* in the mood to buy, and they have already expressed interest in our products. A recent buyer is our highest priority follow-up."

Before we get into the how-to's of mail order follow-up, we'll discuss how the "look" and "flavor" of your promotions should be similar from one mailing or ad to the next so a *recognition factor* begins to work to your advantage.

GIVING YOUR PROMOTIONS A FAMILY RESEMBLANCE

Buyers will start to gain comfort with your ads and mailers *only* if your promotions have certain visual characteristics that tie them all together. If every ad is distinctly different, you may never establish that important identity in the minds of consumers. That family resemblance can be accomplished in various ways:

- Through a distinctive *logo* that is prominently displayed in every one of your promotions
- By use of the same headline *typestyle* that will eventually come to be associated with your company
- When a certain style of product illustration is used repeatedly
- By sticking to the general look you started with, either busy or simple

Figure 9-1 illustrates two logos that were created especially to convey strong consumer identity:

Figure 9-1. A Distinctive Logo

Figure 9-2 provides an example of a headline typestyle used *consistently* by a direct mail advertiser. Remember, the style *doesn't* have to be unusual; it's *the same look time after time* that works to develop consumer familiarity and comfort.

Figure 9-2. Headline Type That Commands Attention

10 REASONS WHY THIS DIFFUSION PUMP IS THE WORLD'S BEST SELLER:

This consistent look should, to the extent possible, be retained *regardless* of the product or service you happen to be offering. It should be present in a mailer selling small appliances and again in your next piece offering silk flowers. This point has to be emphasized when you have graphic designers putting your promotions together.

How long a time should elapse before follow-up is made? Let's take a look at that.

TIMING YOUR FOLLOW-UP EFFORT FOR
OPTIMUM RESULTS

Your follow-up approach should be formalized so each later contact takes place *at a definite time*. In addition to the exact time of follow-up, the *type of contact* also has to be specified. For example, will your second offer be an envelope mailer, a letter, a telephone call, or some other kind of attempt? Further, will it repeat the initial offer or present a different array of products and services?

To a considerable degree, your follow-up to *prospects* has to fit your revenue and profit potential. If your average sale is only $14.95, there would be serious question as to the wisdom of *any* follow-up since your sales and profit results might not cover the cost of another contact. But an average sale of, say, $89.95 or more, probably warrants *at least* one more try. As in so many other mail order approaches, *testing* is needed to reveal the best follow-up plan for your specific needs.

A photo equipment promoter averages a $50 first-time direct mail sale. When a proprietary list is used (previous buyers of mail order photo supplies), the plan illustrated in Figure 9-3 dictates follow-up.

Figure 9-3

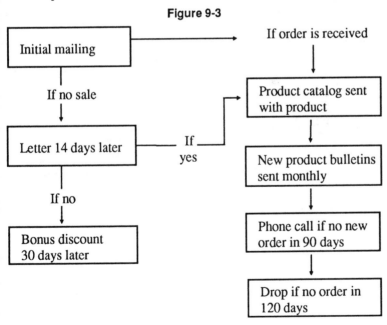

This firm is willing to invest in two follow-up attempts to nonbuyers for this reason: the $50 first-time sale will be just the *beginning* of that consumer's buying pattern. The company typically totals $280 for each mail order buyer over a period of two years. As you can see, they drop customers *and* prospects who are dormant for four consecutive months.

To obtain maximum impact, the *first* follow-up should go out no later than 30-days after the initial offer and preferably before that. Quick follow-up helps assure that the prospect will still recall your initial offer, thus contributing to the cumulative effect that does so much to develop consumer familiarity and comfort.

For *buyers*, there is no such thing as following up too quickly! You will do well if you lavish as much attention as you possibly can on your priceless customers and *don't stop* until well after *they* stop!

We'll turn to the various ways follow-up can be handled.

EFFECTIVE METHODS FOR GETTING BACK IN TOUCH

A logical, sensible, and perhaps obvious rule for guiding follow-up is; *spend less on the second contact than you did on the initial offer*. That means, if you sent a classic Magic Six mailing to first present your offer, go to a comparatively simple format for your follow-up. The reason is purely economic.

A notable exception to that rule occurs in programs designed to *attract inquiries*. In such a case, an initial promotion, whether it's an ad or mailer, is focused on flushing out the prospects who may buy *later*. So it makes perfect sense to send the more powerful piece to those individuals or companies you can classify as qualified leads. Thus, *the follow-up becomes the front-line seller* in most inquiry-generating programs.

In conventional programs, you have a choice of these follow-up methods:

- Letter
- Self-mailer
- Envelope mailing (in cases where the first promotion was a media ad)

- Telemarketing (when your offer is at a high enough dollar level to support a calling program)

Again, which method to use is a matter of dollars and cents. If you are dealing with a large proprietary *consumer* list—and the size of your average sale justifies a follow-up—a simple letter definitely makes most sense. A small average sale, and/or a compiled list, probably does not warrant any kind of follow-up effort.

In selling to business firms, any of the four follow-up methods can be a legitimate choice *if* your average sale is sufficient and the number of prospects is manageable. The truth is, sales—can be made to companies over a longer period of time and in larger dollar amounts, so they demand a little different follow-up strategy than consumers do.

Many mail order operators believe strongly in "turning up the heat" on follow-ups. More about that now.

DEVELOPING HARD-HITTING
FOLLOW-UP APPROACHES

If a consumer or business firm failed to respond to your initial offer, why not sell a little harder in the follow-up? That certainly *is* a valid question, especially if you only plan just one follow-up.

A group that promotes self-improvement courses uses a follow-up circular that opens with this blockbuster copy:

Anyone who can't make money with our program may be condemned to being a "wage-earner" for life!

Thank Heaven that's not YOU!

You've already proved to me that you are ambitious and have a strong desire to *make it* in life. I knew that when you recently inquired about our remarkable program. Your letter told me you are not happy with your career . . . *or the money you are earning*!

This letter goes on to urge the consumer to act now and stop further procrastination.

Promotions to *companies*, which tend to be longer-term programs consisting of more follow-up contacts, are of course gentler in tone, or *should* be! They depend more on developing familiarity and increasing inducements than on provocative copy. Mel Silver sells research services to companies. He explains his firm's follow-up approach this way:

> "Our program can cost a company between $4,000 and $10,000, so we're willing to stick with a follow-up program for up to 18 months, with bimonthly contacts by mail and telephone. It's a low-key cultivation process that is definitely low pressure. By the end of the first six months, these prospects know us, and most are beginning to trust us.
>
> "Each contact we make is intended to convey information, *not* high pressure the prospect into a buying decision. In essence, we believe in educating a company so they'll understand exactly what we offer, and why they need our services."

Two radically different follow-up philosophies. Here's yet another one, oriented to selling products to consumers. It's a follow-up method used by a company selling security systems to homeowners. Gina Henkel, the firm's direct response manager, says:

> "Follow-ups continue for six months—or until the consumer asks us to stop. Once a month we send a simple mailer consisting of a letter, a reply card, and a premium insert. Each insert improves the offer a little from the month before. One time we'll offer a free fire alarm; the next time we'll give buyers an intercom at no extra cost. We gradually break down buyer resistance. Our final contact is a phone call. It's our final attempt to set up a close."

When *can* telemarketing be used in a direct marketing program? Here are the facts.

USING TELEMARKETING TO CREATE NEW SALES

You can spend a fortune on putting out the most powerful imaginable mailer, or the most commanding media ad or TV spot, and none of them can match the pure selling power of a *personal contact* by telephone. While you can certainly cover more ground with mailers and ads, the telephone virtually guarantees you contact with the person who does the buying.

Telemarketing will never take the place of massive promotions involving millions of prospects, but it definitely can compete with programs involving up to 10,000 prospects. The cost per hundred of telemarketing can compare favorably because of the higher closing ratios in direct calling.

Mail order sales are obtained by telephone in the following situations:

- In business-to-business or consumer programs where the potential sale is large enough to absorb the cost of calling. In consumer programs, the leads should be qualified (proprietary list) and the number of names manageable.

- To revive dormant customers in either business-to-business *or* consumer programs. In most cases, inactive buyers are simply too valuable to lose without at least one personal contact.

- In retail sales, telemarketing can be combined effectively with mailings to guarantee high turnouts at customer-only special events.

Actually, the only real exclusion would be a huge compiled consumer list, although they are occasionally covered by phone as well.

You can do a quick, reasonably precise check to find out whether or not telemarketing is a practical choice for you by going through these points.

- Can the costs of calling be absorbed? For long-distance calling, an 800 WATS line, or comparable service, is needed to keep costs under control.

  One more word about that: If your promotions offer a toll-free 800 for customer ordering convenience, it *has to be* accompanied by a *dedicated outbound* WATS line for your telemarketer's use. If you have such a two-line setup, by all means *avoid* having your outbound telemarketer serve the dual role of *taking inbound orders*! Invariably, orders come in while that person is busy calling out, and chaos results.

- Your caller will run a minimum of $4 to as much as $10 per hour. Under the best conditions in a consumer program, the telemarketer will be actually able to *reach* six prospects an hour or so and should close three. In a business program, figure on reaching three decision makers each hour and closing one.

  About four solid hours a day of calling can be expected. That gives you 12 sales per day in a consumer program and 4 a day if you contact businesses.

- Scheduling has to be carefully thought out. In consumer calling, people can be reached with fair success between 6 P.M. and 9 P.M. Calls to businesses are, of course, strictly daytime contacts. And don't forget to consider different time zones if you promote nationally.

- Program controls will do two things for you: (1) provide daily data on calling progress and (2) give you the kind of figures you need to evaluate the payback of telemarketing. Recommended control forms are provided later in this chapter.

More than a few mail order companies have used calling for follow-up and then expanded this approach to make it a major revenue producer.

The following pages provide materials that should be helpful to you in your follow-up telemarketing program.

SAMPLE SCRIPT FOR TELEMARKETING FOLLOW-UP

You want follow-up calls to flow as naturally as possible, and you definitely want them as *brief* as you can get them, so more calls can be made each day. For those reasons, it's good practice to have a new telemarketer work from a script at first—until complete comfort is reached by the caller.

A call like the following one should take no more than a couple of minutes, or somewhat longer if the telemarketer is successful in getting a commitment. This script is used by a mail order company selling office machines to local firms. In this particular case, the call is made between 30 and 60 days after the initial mailer is delivered:

> Telemarketer: Gets the targeted buyer on the line, introduces himself, then says:
>
> "You may remember a mailer we sent to you describing some specials we were offering on fax machines.
>
> "I'd like to tell you briefly about a situation that may make a purchase extremely attractive to you. We're in a position where we have to sell the remaining few machines left in stock.
>
> "We'll give you, at no charge, three rolls of paper if you order the top-of-the-line unit today. And you get the same advertised sale price of $695.
>
> "Can I reserve a machine for you? I can call back later and get your purchase order number."

Again, a follow-up call like this is designed to get *right to the point and cover as many prospects as possible*. There is *no* qualifying, and detailed descriptions of the machine are given by the telemarketer *only* if specific questions are asked by the prospect. It is assumed that a certain number of firms out there *are in the market for a machine* and that a simple call is all it takes to identify those buyers.

FORMS THAT HELP KEEP FOLLOW-UP
ACTION ON TRACK

As your telemarketer follows up prospects, those who decide to buy should be formally noted so the purchase can be properly fulfilled. In a business-to-business program, you may also want to keep a record of every call so a database can be established. It may not pay to take the same pains in a consumer program since nonbuyers are dropped much more quickly in favor of new lists.

Figure 9-4 provides a form that can be used for documenting sales made through follow-up calling *and* for building a record of business prospects.

Figure 9-4

FOLLOW-UP TRACKING FORM

Date: _____   Name of Telemarketer: _____

                           Prospect Source (list): _____

Prospect Name: _____

Address: _____

City: _____ State: _____ Zip: _____

Telephone: ( ): _____

Buyer Name: _____ Title: _____

Check Here If Sale: [   ]

Purchase Information or Other Comments:_____
_____
_____
_____

Purchase Order Number: _____
_____
_____
_____

Promised Delivery Date:_____
_____
_____

Further Follow-up Instructions:_____
_____
_____
_____

One other form is needed in a good follow-up program. It will answer these crucial questions:

- Is my telemarketer closing as effectively as possible?

- Are a sufficient number of calls being made daily?

- Is enough daily time being spent on the phone?

- Most important, does it *pay* to continue telemarketing?

The *"Daily Call Tally Sheet"*, illustrated in Figure 9-5 will provide a recap of daily calling activity.

Each horizontal line represents *one day* of telephone activity. Here's how to use the tally sheet:

DATE	Today's date.
TOTAL CALLS TODAY	How many times the tele-marketer of actually *dialed* prospect numbers today, whether they were contacted or not
PRESENTATIONS	How many of the numbers dialed resulted in *presentations* today.
CLOSED	How many prospects agreed to buy today.
AMOUNT	The total of today's phone orders.

You now have a simple but effective method for analyzing the progress and impact of telephoning on a day-to-day basis.

Now let's delve into a question asked by almost every new mail order entrepreneur: At what point should nonbuyers be dropped from a prospect list?

WHEN TO GIVE UP ON INACTIVE PROSPECTS

As mentioned earlier, there is definitely a payoff when you establish your company and its products in the minds of prospects. Repeated exposures most assuredly *will* win over buyers who hesitate at first.

Figure 9-5

DAILY CALL TALLY SHEET				
Date	Total Calls Today	Presentations Today	Closed Today	Amount of Sales Today
———— ———— ———— ———— ————	———— ———— ———— ————	———— ———— ———— ————	———— ———— ———— ————	-$———— -$———— -$———— -$———— -$————
Weekly Totals				$
———— ———— ———— ————	———— ———— ———— ————	———— ———— ———— ————	———— ———— ———— ————	-$———— -$———— -$———— -$———— -$————
Weekly Totals				$
———— ———— ———— ————	———— ———— ———— ————	———— ———— ———— ————	———— ———— ———— ————	-$———— -$———— -$———— -$———— -$————
Weekly Totals				$
———— ———— ———— ————	———— ———— ———— ————	———— ———— ———— ————	———— ———— ———— ————	-$———— -$———— -$———— -$———— -$————
Weekly Totals				$
———— ———— ———— ————	———— ———— ———— ————	———— ———— ———— ————	———— ———— ———— ————	-$———— -$———— -$———— -$———— -$————

Notes: _____

_____

_____
_____

But the big question is, how long should you persist in the effort to sell those prospects? There are different answers for business-to-business and consumer programs:

- In selling to companies, the cultivation process can go on for a long time indeed. When your product or service is of high dollar value, it can be good strategy to keep trying for up to two years—*if you are certain that your business prospects have a basic need for what you are offering.*

- In consumer markets, if you are selling low-priced items, you are dealing with a virtually inexhaustible supply of prospects—even if they come from more highly qualified proprietary lists. So it doesn't pay to keep banging away at the same list the way a stubborn prospector continually pans for little grains of gold in the same old stream.

- When you sell higher-priced goods or services to consumers, cultivating sales over a longer term is advised.

One factor that dictates that advice is this: Your cost to rent a list for unlimited use can get out of hand. For example, a major list broker charges this way:

For 10,000 *consumers* who recently purchased
mail order gifts (names provided on labels) $620.00

For one additional set of labels with the same
10,000 names $295.00

For one year of unlimited promotions to that list
of 10,000 prior buyers (names provided on
computer disk) $1,550.00

Is it worth $1,550.00 to mail repeatedly to that same list over a period of one year? If it's a consumer list, even if they bought gifts by mail order, highly doubtful. Many experts are convinced you'd reach a point of steeply declining returns after the *second* mailing. So you are probably better off buying two sets of labels, then switching to a *new* prospect population. In this case, *one follow-up* would be the answer.

But in selling to *companies*, you can put together your *own* list far more easily than you can for consumers. In addition to that advantage, firms are much more responsive to long-term cultivation than are consumers. They move less often; tend to stick with the same buying patterns longer, and are generally more loyal to selected vendors.

As a rule of thumb, if your average sale to business firms *or* upscale consumer is:

Up to $50	Follow up for 3 months before dropping
$51 to $100	Follow up for 6 months before dropping
$101 to $200	Follow up for 9 months before dropping
$201 to $500	Follow up for 1 year before dropping
$501 to $2,000	Follow up for 18 months before dropping
$2,001 and up	Follow up for 2 years before dropping

Remember, these are the most *general* kind of guidelines. Once again, *your own testing* should be done to reveal what is right for your mail order needs.

Dormant buyers justify extra concern *if* annual purchases average $150 or so. Declining sales activity, whether consumer *or* business, should trigger one or more personal letters from you, and if that doesn't get action, a telephone call. A suddenly inactive customer shouldn't be allowed to sit more than 90 days before concerted follow-up is made.

When you have occasion to talk directly to prospects, as you would when you use the telephone to follow up, you'll face a variety of situations that you *will* have to deal with in the interest of good service. Here's how to do it with ease.

MAKING THE MOST OF COMPUTER LETTERS

Many of today's most modest personal computers give you the ability to rapidly generate highly responsive follow-up letters to prospects and customers. Here are just a few of the questions you'll be asked as you proceed in business:

- "Is the #788C TV stand available in white?"

- "Will the brass swans still be available in February?"

And so forth. After a while, you'll be able to group inquiries like those so they fit rather neatly into categories. For example, *delivery information, product specifications, complaints, and so on.* If you try to create a brand new letter for each question, you'll never have time to do anything else. And if you use form letters, you may look unresponsive and impersonal. Even worse, questions may not get answered properly.

Following up questions that come in as a result of a promotion can be built around "stock" letters that reside in the memory of a small computer. A word processing program then enables you to type in the pertinent data, print the letter, and get it mailed immediately. Your objective is to turn out a letter that *looks* as if it was typed especially for the inquiring prospect

Here's an example of a stock letter. This particular one deals with product specifications. It responds to a prospect who received your promotion and has questions about a certain product. It's flexible enough to cover a range of similar situations. Underlines represent words or phrases you have to fill-in to complete the letter:

Dear _____ :

Your inquiry about our _____ is appreciated. We are certain you would find this item even more appealing in person than it is in the brochure you received!

Specifications provided to us by the manufacturer are as follows:

_____

_____

_____.

If that does not provide sufficient data, we recommend this:

Send the enclosed request and we will send you a _____ for your approval. If the item does not please you in every way, simply return it in good condition, in its original packing, and an immediate refund will be made to you.

We hope this arrangement is satisfactory and look forward to serving you.

Sincerely,

_____

P.S. We **won't** forget to enclose your free gift. It's yours to keep . . . even if you decide to return your new_____!

Keep a copy of each stock letter you create. Arrange them by category in a three-ring binder so you can rapidly access the right ones in your computer when you sit down to handle correspondence.

Getting out customer orders is very much part of follow-up. That's our next topic.

FILLING CUSTOMER ORDERS PROMPTLY AND PROFESSIONALLY

If you have ever purchased by mail order, you know how exciting it can be to finally receive the item you fell in love with through a picture in a circular or catalog. At that big moment, a purchaser will either be gratified about the transaction or disappointed. Whichever emotion prevails will be directed to the mail order company.

When viewed in that context, delivery is clearly *the most important follow-up you can make*.

You can't very well improve the product or service you sell; it is what it is. But you *can* take steps to heighten the impact on customers when your packages are received and opened. Here are a few ideas on how to do that.

- Get orders out just as fast as you possibly can. Quick turnaround puts your product or service in a buyer's hands when excitement and anticipation are still at a very high level.

   You may want to make sure that a customer check clears before sending off an order—especially if the item's value creates a significant risk to you. That wait can create a delay of two weeks or so. But there is *no* reason to hold up delivery beyond that time.

- Enclose a letter to your buyer that makes these points:

   We appreciate your order.

   If everything isn't just right, let us know.

   We look forward to serving you again in the near future.

- Include *new offer inserts* and an *order form* in the delivery! Remember, the best prospect is a recent buyer.

- Even if your customer saw your satisfaction guarantee in your original promotion, send another one with the delivery.

- Finally, pack the order neatly and securely. This tells your customer, "We value this product as much as you do and want it to reach you in perfect shape."

    One more point about packing orders should be made here: *Neat and secure* does not mean *expensive*. You should take special measures to assure the endurance of a package during the mailing process, but fancy packaging can and should be eliminated if it represents any extra cost to you.

Next, how the most successful mail order operators conduct their programs. We'll look at small- and big-scale promotions and the keys they use to get consistently profitable results.

CHAPTER 10

CLASSIC MAIL ORDER PROGRAMS YOU CAN USE AS MODELS

Reading about the how-to's of mail order *will* help you get your own solid program underway, but there is nothing as profitable as looking at the secrets of seasoned pros in the field. In various mail order offers, there are certain devices that make the difference between just getting by and setting sales records.

Success keys might be copy approaches, free gift ideas, follow-up procedures, or other tactics that turn ordinary products and services into phenomenal money-makers.

In this chapter we'll examine an array of classic mail order campaigns and what makes them winners year after year. In most cases, we'll briefly review the company background; the product or service; the firm's objective; problems to be solved; the offer; and most important, *what the program's success keys are.*

HOW A HIGH-TECH PRODUCT IS SUCCESSFULLY SOLD BY MAIL

Background

One of the most intriguing and wildly profitable mail order programs *ever* used in a business-to-business environment was devised by a small West Coast computer software maker. After only 12 years in business the two founders sold the company, walking away with checks totaling $13 million.

Product

A software system for mainframe computers is priced at about $700. Its functions are well defined, and documentation provided with the package is comparatively easy to use. Chief advantages of the system are time saving for the data processing manager and generation of certain reports not produced by other economical means.

Problems

The software maker is unable to sell the package through field sales representatives due to the tremendous costs involved. This situation forces the firm to try and have prospects run a demo of the system so its report capabilities can be evaluated by potential buyers. Time saving can't be demonstrated convincingly through the demo, so that important attribute will have to be described as graphically as possible.

Cost, while reasonable for a large computer software system, may also be a problem if prospects fail to demo the system. Its strengths might not look big enough to justify the system's price.

Offer

Mail order is selected as the primary promotional medium. One clear advantage to mailing in this case is the easy identification of the market since mainframe user lists are readily available and manager names can also be acquired. The total audience numbers only about 5,000 firms, so a high-intensity program of monthly mailings and telephone follow-up is planned.

Success Keys

To get the interest of data processing managers, *visual gimmicks* are created to get the time saving point across. Figure 10-1 is one example; The cartoon portrays a "time machine," thus dramatizing this leading strength of the system. Such an approach draws prospect managers into reading more about the product.

Figure 10-1. A Visual Gimmick That Helps Sell Intangibles

Another success key is to take the sting out of the $700 price tag by equating the figure to a tiny daily expense. To accomplish that, the package is advertised in mailers as:

$2 A DAY SOFTWARE

A third key is to offer data processing managers a substantial free gift just for trying the demonstration package. This is vital since a trial demands the time of busy people. The gift is sent to a prospect when a printout of the demo program is received by the selling firm, which proves the trial took place.

Finally, telephone follow-up proves extremely valuable for these reasons: prospects who need more technical data have an opportunity to get the answers they need to make a decision. Also, the call is an ideal way to prod procrastinators gently into trying the demo that is often languishing on a shelf. It should be noted that very few prospects actually throw the demo package away since it looks and

feels valuable, containing a tape, a small starter manual, and the offer
of a very nice gift.

Here's how a small publisher turned things around quickly.

TURNING FEATURES INTO BENEFITS CREATES
A MAIL ORDER SUPERSTAR

Background

A Midwest-based publisher of financial consulting programs moved
from the edge of bankruptcy to hefty profits in only six months by
transforming dull features into captivating benefits.

Service

This company teaches individuals how to obtain funding for business
and real estate ventures and how to advise others on getting loans.
Training packages are priced in the $69 to $279 range and consist of
manuals, audio tapes, and videos.

Problems

Being a service, there are no compelling visual elements that would
attract prospects. As a result, ads are all type; there are no photos or
illustrations. *Headlines* have to carry almost the entire load of an ad's
appeal.

Offer

To reach large numbers of potential program buyers economically,
small print ads in mail order–oriented national magazines are run.
Direct mail is utilized only to sell newly developed programs to
existing customers.

Test cable TV spots have been moderately successful, and this
approach is to be expanded. Broadcast provides an excellent medium
for telling success stories through testimonials.

Success Keys

Headlines used early in the company's development stressed *features*
of the program and failed dismally. Response levels were barely high
enough to keep the company in business. Then headlines were revised

to emphasize the financial *benefits* that could accrue to program buyers. Examples of changes are:

- The old headline *Directory of Government Grants* became

  GET $25,000.00 FOR ONE PHONE CALL

- The old headline *Learn How to Apply for Big Real Estate Loans* became

  $MILLIONS ON REQUEST

- The old headline *Start Your Own Financial Telephone Hotline* became

  $3,000.00 A WEEK SELLING FACTS BY PHONE

Results were immediate and dramatic. Responses shot up an average of 40 percent, and the firm was instantly put on a profitable course.

While these revised headlines are really overblown promises of quick riches—and as such may be close to the ethical line—they *do* illustrate how boring features can easily be converted to powerful benefits that *get the job done*.

An innovative mail order campaign for a kitchen device follows.

MAKING SMALL APPLIANCES A *MUST* FOR CONSUMERS

Background

While countless retailers and mail order firms hammer the public with almost desperate discount offers on small appliances, DAK, a California merchandiser, sells consumers by educating them. In this instance, it has created a thick booklet that's *devoted entirely* to one kitchen device!

Product

This is a bread baking machine that DAK claims will automatically turn out top-quality loaves, high in nutrition, with no additives. It's offered at $129.95. This model is private labeled for DAK. Competitive units range generally from $120 to $180.

Problems

The main difficulty in effectively selling a large number of machines like the bread baker is consumer awareness: At first glance, the unit resembles a coffee grinder, a juicer, or a food processor. It does not impart a clear visual image as to what it *does*.

Also, the bread baker's price *demands* a sales effort that goes beyond a mere discounted price. Its capabilities *have to be sold*. Normal-sized media ads would never provide sufficient space to tell the story the way it has to be told in this case.

Offer

Without question, one of the most extraordinary approaches ever used to sell an appliance like the bread baker, DAK has prepared a *66-page booklet* that is devoted to this machine. It's called a *Guide to Automatic Bread Making*.

Success Keys

DAK's booklet contains 58 "Great Bread Recipes." Consumers are hooked on what the machine does instead of what it *is*. Features and price are no longer the only points to talk about. One look through the pages of DAK's booklet *will convince* anybody who loves home-made bread and wants to start baking at home without the usual hassle associated with that task.

To get the no-hassle point across, one page in the booklet explains the steps involved in manual bread making. It informs the reader that any of the 58 recipes *can* be done by hand, but doing so is "tedious."

How do some very effective mail order programs manage to grab the eyes of buyers? Here's one way to do it.

HOW THE QUESTION APPROACH MAKES CERTAIN OFFERS ALMOST IRRESISTIBLE

Background

A real estate company doing business in U.S. southern states recruits agents constantly. Growth and turnover keep demand for salespeople at a high level. At the same time, ads are run to stimulate listings traffic.

Problems

Conservative copy approaches often did not attract a single call in either need category. The typical tone of those ads was:

> Join the real estate leader and sell your home fast

Certainly neither is very compelling, so radical changes were made to headlines. To draw readers into responding, *provocative questions* were adopted for headlines. The result: a rapid improvement in both phases of the recruitment program.

Success Keys

By understanding what motivates a certain group of consumers, the questions *they* are likely to ask become evident and can be used as headlines. A strategy like this can produce tremendous curiosity in the reader, which will often lead that person into the copy. Handled correctly, the copy does *not* answer the question directly, but gives *just enough* information to trigger a call, thus producing a good lead.

In their agent recruitment campaign, these questions/headlines are used:

> Can you make huge income as a real estate *beginner*?
>   And
> How much can you make *this year* in real estate?

Again, the supporting body copy does not give specifics. Text for the first ad takes a direction like this:

> You'll be amazed at the breathtaking potential . . . even for new agents! Call me RIGHT NOW and I'll give you figures on how much our new people have earned, and the money *you* are capable of making with our great program in back of you.

Listing ads look like this:

> When will home prices soar out of sight?
>
> Is *your* neighborhood in our "Hot-Home-Selling" zone?
>
> What *kind* of house brings top profits?

For the latter ad, supporting copy reads:

> No matter what you may think of your home, it may be exactly what our clients are looking for! We have *ready, qualified buyers* seeking the features your residence may have. That means top dollars for you. Call me TODAY so we can find out.

Questions work in virtually any kind of direct response promotion. Once you know what's on the mind of your prospect, questions that make strong headlines will pop out.

There *are* best times of year to promote by mail order. Here's how one very accomplished operator sees it.

A FASCINATING STUDY IN MAIL ORDER SEASONAL STRATEGY

Every mail order operator has to be tuned into the strongest selling seasons for his or her product or service. In most markets these are the primary seasons for fruitful promotions:

- Fall season runs from late August through late November.

- Winter season runs from early January through about mid-March.

- Christmas buying is normally in full swing from September through the second week of December.

- For some specialties—such as certain gardening supplies—late December to early January is prime time, along with the early fall of the year.

- Easter, Valentine's Day, Mother's Day, Father's Day, and even Halloween are also profitable times for items that fit those special days. Aside from those buying hotspots, the doldrums can be expected to begin in late March and continue through much of August. Unless you know something that departs from conventional wisdom, that slower period is when *your promotional budget can be reduced*.

Susan DiFino, as noted earlier, designs and manufactures fancy, high-quality garters sold by lingerie retailers, department stores, and bridal shops. She has built the success of her mail order sales program largely *by working her prime selling season to the absolute maximum*. This garter entrepreneur rigidly adheres to a promotion and production schedule that generates peak sales for Mother's Day, Easter, Valentine's Day, and Christmas.

We'll review the type of package Susan mails to her carefully selected prospect list. A letter, a separate reply card, representative sample garters, and color swatches constitute the package sent to prospects. Here is the letter used last Valentine's Day:

Dear (name of garter buyer):

Valentine's Day is coming, and our newly created garter collection is ready for you and your customers.

While women have traditionally worn the garter for good luck, it is considered the sexiest adornment that can grace the female leg. As such, the centuries old garter is enjoying enormous popularity all over the world. Here's a great way for you to cash in on this remarkable trend:

> EXQUISITE DIFINO GARTERS BRING YOUR CUSTOMERS OLD-FASHIONED VALUE, BEAUTY, AND QUALITY. EVERY PIECE WE MAKE IS AS PERFECTLY CRAFTED AS THE ENCLOSED SAMPLES.

> THEY ARE **PROVEN** BEST-SELLERS AND ARE CERTAIN TO BRING **YOU** FAST, PROFITABLE IMPULSE SALES.

DiFino garters are made of fine laces and exclusive hand-formed embellishments. **Each product** is carefully inspected at four different stages of construction. This meticulous quality control virtually assures the utmost in customer satisfaction.

In addition to the superb value inherent in DiFino garters, they bring your store a product deep in romance and tradition. Each product includes the story of how the garter became established as a wedding symbol in fourteenth century England, as it continues to be to this day.

DiFino's objective is to help give your Valentine's Day customers the feeling that their garter purchases are adventures.

We look forward to serving you. Please call, fax, or return the enclosed merchandise request form to me.

Sincerely,

Susan DiFino

Susan DiFino

These ordering instructions are printed on a detachable portion of the merchandise request form:

DiFino gives you a complete program for bigger-than-ever profits

Any purchase of 100 or more garters can be *private labeled*. You provide the labels, DiFino does the rest.

Please check the enclosed garter samples and color swatches. You can mix and match to your heart's content.

Freight is FREE on any order of 100 garters or more.

Delivery is *fast*. Fax or mail your order today, and your merchandise will be shipped just ten days after we receive your request.

To give the product an extra bit of romance, a tag, printed on rich parchment, is attached to each garter. It carries this copy:

Something old, something new, something borrowed, something blue. The garter can be any of the four—or simply for good luck.

In old English custom, guests secretly entered the newlyweds' bedchamber and stole their stockings. By the fourteenth century, only the bride's garter was coveted. Folklore held that the successful "thief" would be the next to marry, so male guests tried to grab the garter. To protect their privacy, the bride and groom began tossing the garter to single men.

The Way to Wear Your Garter
Wear just below the knee with lace facing down, the embellishment on the outside.

Coordinate garter colors and styles with your favorite outfits. An elegant garter is your secret . . . as long as you want to keep it to yourself.

This program is beautifully merchandised, effectively timed, and targeted to precisely the right markets. It *works*!

To continue the theme of making items at home, the important topic of *successfully selling home crafts and hobbies* is now addressed in greater detail.

SELLING HOME CRAFTS AND HOBBIES BY MAIL ORDER CAN BE BIG BUSINESS

Background

Paula Heeter worked at a string of jobs, but never really got pleasure from anything but her unique Christmas tree decorations. Made of a variety of materials, these ornament collections are loved by everybody who sees them. At first the only time Paula had to devote to designing and making her charming angels was evenings and week-ends. Now, five years after starting, she has six part-time people working year-round to turn out enough sets to satisfy holiday season demand.

Product

Ornaments are brightly colored, exquisitely ornate angels taken from illustrations of old European Christmas decorations. They are pack-aged in sets of 6 and 12, retailing for $14.95 and $27.95, respectively. Most work is manual, and the product definitely has a hand-crafted look.

Problems

When Paula first realized that her hobby could be parlayed into a going business, she came to some important conclusions about how it could be sold profitably. First, going direct to retail stores presented one big difficulty: To resell the set of 24 at about $25, a store would have to buy that assortment from Paula for around $10. While a retailer might order fairly large quantities, $10 would simply not provide enough profit to the new manufacturer.

Selling direct to consumers was the answer. Promotional ex-penses might cost more, but the ornament maker would get the full retail price. In addition, she was certain that referrals would produce a substantial number of new buyers every year.

Approach

Christmas tree ornaments are usually purchased during the Novem-ber/December season, but in her first year of operation, Paula decided to work the rest of the year doing two crucially important tasks: building a highly qualified prospect list and stocking enough sets to fill the heavy demand that could be expected in those hot selling months.

There was no more cost-effective way to build a list than by running small classified ads. For starters, Paula selected a group of four women's magazines, each one rich in mail order offers. This simple copy was used in initial test ads:

HEIRLOOM ANGELS

Hand-crafted decorations
from ancient European
Christmas lore.
Free brochure

RARE ORNAMENTS

Magnificent hand-made
angels for generations
of holiday joy.
Free brochure.

COLLECTOR'S ANGELS

You'll treasure these
exquisite replicas of
ancient Christmas tradition.
Free brochure.

Paula's first year proceeded this way: From mid-January to late October, she built a list of 4,270 prospects. These people received a simple brochure showing both assortments. Some 312 consumers ordered sets through the off season. Equally important, a strong list was established. Those who did not respond received a mailing in September. This produced 390 immediate orders, plus an additional 127 orders a little later, many from referrals—very encouraging for her first year in business.

Now into her fifth year, the entrepreneur is at a level of nearly 5,000 sets per year: Gross income is well over $100,000 and growing. Paula still uses the classified ad strategy. She has expanded her ornament line, and prices have risen to fit the value of the product.

Success Keys

Extremely low promotional costs are decidedly the basis of Paula Heeter's progress. She enjoys low overhead by virtue of working at home and using part-time help.

Use of the "Ancient," "Collector's," and "Rare" ad themes provide lots of mystique in a few words. And Paula was right about referrals; nearly half of her sales are now recommended by prior leads.

Many mail order entrepreneurs who plan to target businesses wonder what gets company buyers excited enough to buy. Here's the way one firm does it.

BUILDING APPEAL FOR BUSINESS PRODUCTS AND SERVICES

Generally speaking, companies purchase when they are convinced that:

- Your product or service will save them time and money.

- Your quality is good, and the value is solid.

- You'll be around to back up whatever you sell.

Saving time and money can take various forms. It can focus on the increased productivity of employees, the simplification of job tasks, reduced waste, enhanced safety, and a long list of other improvements.

Solid value doesn't mean you have to come in considerably cheaper than your competition. It means your cost has to be in line and justifiable in terms of the benefits you offer. In fact, many company buyers who experience a seller trying to undercut rivals will realize that shortcuts will have to be taken by that vendor, eventually leading to inferior quality and service somewhere down the line.

Mail order firms can use media ads and direct mail to close sales on items up to a certain price *without* using direct contact such as personal visits or phone calls. That figure can vary according to the product and the audience, but an approximation is $100. Beyond that, you may have to do some personal selling in addition to other efforts—although there *are* exceptions.

Romance enjoys less impact in business environments than it does with consumers. Firms are much more hard-headed, that is, far less impulsive, about what they buy. Tangible trade-offs have to be perceived by company decision makers.

A good example of how to express a mail order sales pitch to companies is this promotion from a commercial coffee service.

We make sure that coffee satisfies your people, and that it's packaged in quantities that give them a boost. That's been *proven* to increase productivity.

Also, we make sure that this fine coffee is convenient to everybody, clerks and top managers alike, so they stay at their work stations.

This is a Total Systems Approach that goes far beyond just installing brewers and supplying coffee. And it costs no more than ordinary coffee services.

In this instance, the concept of merely service as just another coffee vendor wasn't enough. This coffee service has tried hard to comprehend some of the needs of business and then fashioned a service that deals with some of those needs. Through that kind of appeal, the seller doesn't have to rely on having the lowest prices in town in order to compete. The value offered by this particular coffee service is the key.

Now we'll take an in-depth look at how the figures should work in your mail order enterprise.

CHAPTER 11

CALCULATING PROFIT MARGINS, SELLING PRICES, MAILING COSTS, AND OTHER VITAL FINANCIAL FACTORS

More than one mail order expert is sure that success in this business is based on how adeptly dollars are controlled. Big sales don't matter much if profits are devoured by excessive mailing costs, dormant inventory, bad equipment decisions, and other causes of wasted cash. Of course the problem is compounded if profits themselves are too thin.

Sound money-handling is so important to the continued health of your mail order business that two chapters, 11 and 12, are devoted to helping you make the right financial moves and steering clear of the pitfalls that can keep you from the success you are working to achieve.

SETTING SALES EXPECTATIONS

As soon as you can predict results with some degree of accuracy, life gets a lot easier in mail order. For starters, you'll be in a better position to line up your product needs, and that will lead directly to economies in packing materials, employee time, and other factors. Equally important, you will be poised to plan the size of your promotions.

While it's great to be positive and optimistic about how a certain ad or mailing will do, a *realistic outlook is still the best business practice*. For that reason, it makes very good sense to base your expectations on outcomes that other mail order operators have experienced over a period of recent years.

For direct mail programs, predicting results is pretty straightforward since there are three basic *known* items to consider: list quality, the number to be mailed, and the impact and uniqueness of your offer. Today, the following response guidelines hold true:

- Mailing to *prospects* should generate a 0.5 to 1.5 percent response. So a reasonably strong mailing to a good proprietary list of 10,000 can be expected to give you 50 to 150 responses.

- Mailings to *customers* generally yield 3.0 to 7.0 percent, or 300 to 700 responses in a 10,000 mailing.

Mailings *can* sometimes exceed the wildest expectations by bringing in 20 percent responses, or better. But that's definitely the exception and not a normal outcome.

In media promotions, there are *many* more uncertainties and variables, for example, audience size for a particular edition, the location of your ad (or the times it runs), how your offer stands out among competing offers, and so forth. In addition, you have to consider how a first-time ad might compare in pulling power to one that has become familiar to prospects through repeated runs. The result of all these unknowns is this:

> Nobody on earth can even begin to predict what the response will be to a new ad conveying a new offer in a new magazine, newspaper, or broadcast medium.

There are simply *no* reliable ways to estimate what will happen in first-time media promotions. You have to *test* in order to find out. Back in Chapter 4, we covered *cost per response*. When you *do* test your media ad, use this simple method to find out if you're on the right track:

> Divide your responses into the cost of the ad. The answer is your cost per response. If you can comfortably absorb that figure in your profit margin, you made a good media choice.

Once testing has been done, you *will* be able to set expectations intelligently for future media promotions.

Pricing is a somewhat more exact science than media advertising.

ESTABLISHING REALISTIC MAIL ORDER SELLING PRICES

You need a pricing philosophy, a definite position that you stick with over the long haul.

Paul B. Brown of *Inc.* magazine observes that the most important factor in pricing is *consistency*. Mr. Brown says: "you can't be inconsistent. If you're cheap one day, expensive the next, and in the middle every other Thursday, you'll just confuse people." He also believes there is truth in what today's marketing gurus are saying: You can no longer compete solely on price. Customers need speedy delivery, better service, and more quality.

All that points directly at a steady pricing formula that gives you enough profit to back up what you sell and continue your personal and business growth.

True, you have to be competitive. But it's no longer necessary to clobber the competition in every promotion. Phrases such as "Special Sale," "Lowest Wholesale Prices," and the like have been without consumer credibility for years and may not recover in our lifetime.

Products can safely be priced in a range of 100 to 150 percent over cost. That is, a product that costs you $10 would be retailed in your promotion at $20 to $25. "Cost" is the amount your supplier charges you, plus freight or any other costs associated with transferring the goods to your possession.

Obviously, the more unusual or rare your product or service, the more you can charge. And any items created by *you* can usually be priced at the higher end of the range.

Operators selling their own products or services sometimes price too low since hard costs can be difficult to determine. To avoid giving cash away, you are urged to look at other offers similar to yours and set prices accordingly.

Once you establish a mark up percentage that covers *all* costs and yields a comfortable *net profit* (5 to 9 percent), use that number as often as practical. If you use free gifts, two-for-one, or other buying incentives, use those inducements *consistently* so customers don't get into the habit of postponing their purchases until your offer improves!

Use the worksheet in Figure 11-1 to help establish a picture of how your numbers work.

MAIL ORDER COST WORKSHEET

Figure 11-1. Cost Worksheet

Revenue per unit:

Selling Price$————-

Shipping Charges$————

Total Average Order Revenue $————

Cost per unit:

Product/Service Cost$————

Order Processing$————

Shipping$————

Bad Debts$————

Overhead$————

Total Costs $————

Campaign Costs (total costs):

Lists$————

Creative$————

Printing:

Letter	$————
Brochure	$————
Reply Card	$————
Envelope	$————
Media Ad	$————
Other	$————

Printing Subtotal		$———
Mail Preparation	$———	
Postage	$———	
Telemarketing	$———	
Total Campaign Cost		$———

Net Profit:

(Total revenue – total campaign cost) $———

Cost Per Thousand Mailed

(Total campaign costs ÷ pieces mailed × 1,000) $———

You'll need some experience to zero in on fair amounts to allocate for bad debts and order processing, but a good initial guess is 2 to 4 percent for both items *if* you do business strictly on a cash basis. Use 4 to 8 percent if you bill customers.

Now we'll cover a critically important expense category.

WHEN TO USE FIRST CLASS MAIL

Spending premium money to send mailers out first class can be a wise move in *business-to-business* direct mail under certain conditions. Here are three cases where first class can be cost-effective:

- When a mail order program utilizes mailing and telemarketing, it is excellent strategy to mail first, then follow-up with a phone call. To get maximum punch, the call should be made within four days of the time your prospect receives the mailer. The *only* way to count on reasonably precise delivery is to use first class where you can figure on three or four day delivery, as opposed to ten days to two weeks for bulk rate.

- Sensitive dates, such as holidays like Easter and Valentine's Day, may require you to get your offer to retail buyers on exact days. In those cases, first class definitely might pay.

- Invitations to special customer events generally demand first class for this reason: You don't want to mail an invitation too far in advance because people might forget the date of the event. Ideally, an invitation reaches the target four to seven days before the event.

- For invitations, announcements, or mini-promotions, consider using *post cards*. You'll save a bundle of money. For example, a mailing of 50,000 will cost *$5,000 less than first class*, based on prevailing rates!

Back to first class. *Avoid* non-standard sizes since they will probably take longer to deliver and certainly will cost you more to mail. A uniquely shaped promotion may be an eye-catcher, but will cost $5,000 *extra* to mail to a list of 50,000.

If at all possible, *presort* your first class mailing. Even with the extra labor involved, you will still save money and delivery time. A mailing service can handle that task for you.

For all but the most unusual situations, *bulk-rate* is the way to go in direct mail.

CLEARING UP THE MYSTERIES OF BULK-RATE THIRD CLASS MAILINGS

According to some of the heaviest hitters in mail order, bulk-rate promotions are "junk mail," pure and simple. It makes fortunes for them, but they are perfectly comfortable with that undignified description.

Last year, well over *62 billion* pieces of bulk-rate mail were sent. That's about 550 hits on every mailbox in the United States. Some 92 million people—or over 51 percent of American adults—bought goods and services by mail and telephone. It may be called junk mail by senders and recipients alike, but it's pure gold to thousands of mail order operators.

Direct mailers are put off by the rather arcane steps imposed on bulk mailers by the Postal Service. But when you consider the staggering task they face in delivering *160 billion pieces of mail a year* in the United States, they really are not asking terribly much of volume mailers.

Here are the basic steps involved in bulk mailing:

- You need a bulk-rate permit. Cost is $60 per year.

- You have to mail 200 pieces or more at one time to qualify for the bulk-rate, and your destination has to be in the United States.

- You can use any of the postage payment methods illustrated in Figures 11-2, 11-3, and 11-4.

Precanceled stamp. Buy them in rolls of 500 after getting an authorization from your local post office. They *are* more attractive

than the imprints that follow.

Figure 11-2. Example of a Precanceled Stamp

Permit imprint. After you pay one-time fee (over and above the permit fee), your printer can apply the imprint at the same time your

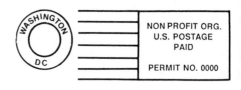

mailing envelope is on the press.

Figure 11-3. Examples of Imprinted Permits

If you decide to buy or lease your own postage meter, you can

imprint bulk-rate mailings yourself.

Figure 11-4. Example of a Meter Imprint

- Correct packaging of groups of envelopes, and sacking those packages, is the step that stops many operators. But after you do the job once, its perceived complexities vanish.

  Your local Post Office can give you an informative booklet called *"Third-Class Mail Preparation"* that takes you through the procedure.

- Fill out a "Statement of Mailing," a form provided by your local Post Office.

- Finally, take your sacks of mail to the nearest Bulk-Rate Acceptance Unit. Call to find out which Post Office in your community has this facility. You *can't* drop a bulk mailing in a mail box!

To qualify for bulk-rate mailings, you can't send handwritten, typed, or any other *personalized* correspondence. Only current dates, headings, salutations, and signatures can be personalized. Be careful about this, since bulk-rate mail is often inspected.

You *can* arrange for mail return service if you pay an extra fee, which is a good idea if you want to keep track of customer address changes. Whether you request return service or not, bulk-rate mail *must* carry a return address.

One more fact to bear in mind is this: You can't mix your mailings with sacks from another mailer.

Regular Bulk Rate

SINGLE PIECE @ 25 CENTS			SAVINGS PER 1,000
Save 8.3 cents	Basic	@ 16.7 cents	$ 83.00
Save 8.8 cents	Basic ZIP + 4	@ 16.2 cents	$ 88.00
Save 11.8 cents	5-Digit	@ 13.2 cents	$ 118.00
Save 12.3 cents	5-Digit ZIP + 4	@ 12.7 cents	$ 123.00
Save 12.8 cents	ZIP + 4 Barcoded	@ 12.2 cents	$ 128.00
Save 14.9 cents	Carrier Route	@ 10.1 cents	$ 149.00

Figure 11-5. Bulk Rate Savings Chart

Again, it *does pay* to use bulk-rate. Figure 11-5 shows you just how much money is at stake.

Alternative mail delivery service is fast gaining in popularity among large and small mail order promoters. Here's more about it.

HOME DELIVERY CAN SAVE YOU MONEY AND TIME

A pizza restaurant owner decided to send out a discount coupon special that would tie in with a city-wide food festival. The decision was made late, and the entire promotion would have to be executed and delivered in just over a week, a task that looked utterly impossible. But the promotion *did* get printed, and it *did* get into the hands of neighborhood residents a safe three days before the critical festival weekend.

The key to making it happen was *home delivery.* It works this way:

This promotion was printed in just two days. The discount coupons were then placed in clear plastic bags and hand delivered to homes in selected neighborhoods. Trained and supervised crews fanned out and rapidly hooked the bags onto home and apartment doorknobs. Only *one day* was needed to hit over 2,000 residences.

Alternative mail delivery services operate in most larger cities. Most have design and printing capabilities so promotions can be completed quickly. These services claim to offer costs that beat bulk-rate by up to 40 percent. Scheduling flexibility and seven day-per-week service are their strongest points. Carriers cover the same routes used by postal service people, so precise geographic selectivity is one more advantage.

There is evidence that consumers are more apt to read door-hung promotions than items they receive by standard mail. You don't often see a bag on your front door, so it does command attention.

You can share space in a plastic bag with other promoters to save yet more money. Make sure that the alternative service you select has strong supervisory capabilities so you're sure that all of your pieces are going where they should be going.

A brief word now about how to address envelopes the right way for conventional mailings.

THE ONLY WAY TO ADDRESS DIRECT MAIL

Setting up addresses improperly can cost you plenty through mailing delays. Whether you use first class *or* bulk rate, here's the right address format:

BARRY Z MASSER
326 W MERCER SUITE 307
SEATTLE WA 98119

To conform with the requirements of Post Office computerized optical character reading equipment, use *all caps*, eliminate periods and commas, use standard abbreviations, and make sure zip codes are correct. By all means, review the latest Postal Service how-to publications before you get too far in preparing a campaign.

Any information that is not related to the address, such as the name and title of an addressee, goes *above* the address block, like this:

ATTN ROBERT MCHUGHES
VP FINANCE
209 ORSON CT SUITE 70
ST CLOUD GA 23022-0202

You can't assume that list brokers and mailing services get the addressing operation perfectly right. It's up to you to make sure.

Next, consider this possible opportunity to save money on packaging.

REPACKAGING TO SAVE MONEY AND
BOOST YOUR IMAGE

Products you buy for mail order promotions may come to you in some of these forms:

- In individual boxes that could be much too large and heavier than they have to be. Excess size and weight *will* cost you more in mailing expense.

- The box of an overseas manufacturer may be designed for foreign markets and thus may not be relevant to U.S. consumers in terms of language and graphics.

- Your supplier's name and address might be prominently displayed on the box, but you could be interested in keeping the source a private matter.

Repackaging products will solve all these problems. It *does* pay if you can negotiate a better price with your supplier by purchasing the items in bulk. A *manufacturer* might agree to cut prices a little bit if they can ship your order without individual boxes. A distributor or jobber probably won't want to bother with such an arrangement.

If you can work out a bulk purchase deal with your source, you can repack the items in a simpler, more efficient (but equally protective) box and put your *own* company identification on it. That can not only save money on shipping, but will also serve to publicize *you*, not some overseas factory.

Selecting the best ways to ship customer orders is covered next.

DELIVERY METHODS THAT HELP GENERATE PROFITS

In mail order your shipping department has to be considered a *source of profits*. Those who regard shipping as a necessary evil, getting by with marginal equipment and minimum attention to the task, will be prone to financial losses that can reach astounding totals over time.

These three factors have to be the focus of concern in your shipping operation: cost of shipment; the difference between the many available shipping services, and how long it will take to get orders to your customers.

You have a rich selection of shipping services at your fingertips in most metropolitan areas. Check the *"Delivery Services"* classification in your Yellow Pages directory to get the complete list. For each type of delivery you'll make in your program, there is one or more service that can handle it best and most economically. It is recommended procedure to check out *each one* so you'll know which ones to depend on for certain kinds of packages.

Harvey Schoener of Detecto Scale Company shed some light on today's most efficient shipping systems for small- to medium-sized firms:

> One vital issue is equipment. Mechanical scales *are* usually accurate enough, but are subject to parallax. And weight readings have to be interpreted then referenced on a chart. Both steps invite mistakes. Also, even the best operators sometimes have to make judgment calls and often prefer to err on the side of *extra* postage so packages won't be bounced back.
>
> Digital scales take the guesswork out of the process. They automatically calculate weight and zip destinations to pin-point cost. They're available in a wide variety of sizes to meet individual requirements.

Great deals on used mechanical scales can represent false economies. Their potential inaccuracies can end up costing far more than a small new digital unit.

Schoener describes two package mailing *systems* a mail order operator can use:

> One, called a *registration system*, is adequate for small firms. Here, a meter is set up for a specific delivery service, UPS, for example. A package is weighed; the stamp is printed, indicating cost; and the stamp is then placed on the package. This system is subject to the same errors mentioned earlier, but it has sufficed for countless lower-volume operations.
>
> *Manifesting* is state of the art in shipping room technology. One version is *scale based* which is easy to use and oriented to small- and medium-sized mail order operations. A digital scale is used to generate a stamp, precisely figured for zip code and carrier of choice. Day-end reports on mailing activity are also provided.
>
> *PC-based manifesting* is highly sophisticated, designed for volume of 300 to 10,000 or more packages per day. These systems can do rate shopping, bar coding, label printing, and archiving.

For starters, use the registration system or scale-based manifesting for your shipping room. Talk to as many of the mailing scale firms as possible *before* you make any equipment commitments.

Now, here is more about the equipment you need to get started in mail order.

INTELLIGENTLY HANDLING EQUIPMENT ACQUISITIONS

When you conduct a home-based mail order enterprise, you should *not* have to grapple with big outlays for equipment. Whatever funds you have to invest should go mainly to *producing revenue*. That means spending for lists, ad space, and promotion preparation, *not* equipment.

We'll assume you already have the basic office necessities such as a desk (a kitchen table can suffice for now), a chair, filing space, and supplies such as paperclips. That leaves the devices you'll have to use to get out mailings and deliveries:

In Preparing Mailers . . .

- The purchase of a computer with word processing software (which can sometimes handle some list maintenance as well) and a printer capable of producing letter-quality output should be considered.

- You certainly *can do without a computer* in the early stages. Many successful mail order operators still maintain lists, generate correspondence, and keep records *manually*. If you decide to use a mailing service, you can get by without a computer much more easily.

- A copier can be a major convenience. But the expense might be unnecessary if you can get whatever duplicates you need at a local shop for about 10 cents each. Once more, the cost *can* be saved initially without significant ill effect.

- ˉFax machines can double as copiers, but fax capabilities make sense only if you market to businesses, since few consumers own them. These machines can also be useful in communicating rapidly with vendors. Here again, you might be better off at first using an outside service if fax will be seldom used.

In Preparing Mailings and Deliveries . . .

- *A tape dispenser for sealing packages.* Good ones give you easy one-hand operation and use rolls of water-activated tape. A sponge on the dispenser dampens the adhesive side of the tape. The outside of the tape can be imprinted with your company name and logo.

- *A worktable* that gives you a big, flat, solid surface for packaging. About 72 inches by 36 inches should be sufficient.

- *A postage scale/meter,* as described earlier. These can be leased, a good idea in case you have to upgrade due to growth of your business. Remember to get *digital* equipment if budget permits.

- **Forms such as labels, packing slips and invoices.** Before you buy forms, work out the details of how your system is to work. More about this is considered in Chapter 13.

- *Packaging materials* such as plastic bags, boxes, foam "peanuts," and other items. Before you can identify precisely what you'll need, you have to know what kind of products you'll be sending.

Companies that sell packaging materials *will help you work out your packaging techniques.* That's part of their service to customers. If at all possible, use a *commercial packaging company* instead of a retail packaging supply store. The price differences can be enormous!

With these items in place—or the availability of outside services that can provide them to you at reasonable rates—you *are in business.*

Savings can also be achieved on the vital accounting function, covered now.

SIMPLE SYSTEMS FOR TRACKING INCOME AND EXPENSES

When transactions take place almost every working day—as they do in a mail order business—you need some record-keeping shortcuts. The last thing you want is a growing stack of memos that have to be deciphered and posted once a month. You can bet that some of those sales, purchases, and credits will be impossible to comprehend a week or two after the fact.

A "write-it-once" bookkeeping system simplifies the entry of transactions. Such a system is designed for trouble-free *daily* posting. At the conclusion of each day, you write the dollar amount of each transaction down *once* in the correct column and presto! it automatically comes up everywhere it should be.

Periodically, an accountant can refer to your daily bookkeeping and easily create tax reports, profit and loss statements, plus any other financial records required in your business. That person's rate is held to a minimum by virtue of your simple daily entries.

Complete write-it-once bookkeeping systems are available in most office supply stores. They come in all shapes and sizes, but all are intended to make the life of an entrepreneur more organized.

Daily entries help to assure that transactions are still clearly recalled and virtually guarantee that some don't get lost as they would if they sat waiting for any length of time. These systems *do* save time, money and untold grief.

In case you get into a position where you *bill* customers for their mail order purchases, and payment doesn't arrive when it should, these letters might help you.

SAMPLE COLLECTION LETTERS FOR SLOW-PAYING CUSTOMERS

In consumer mail order, you probably won't get involved in billing customers. But in selling to business firms, it's quite likely you'll do some invoicing. As you know, not all companies pay their bills promptly, and slow or no-payment can absolutely wreak havoc on your profit picture. These sample letters can serve as models for versions you may need in speeding up payment:

First Letter to Past Due Account

Dear _____:

Your order for _____ was shipped via UPS on July 24. We trust it was received by you promptly and in perfect condition. So that you can check the accuracy of your records, that shipment was billed on our Invoice #_____ in the amount of $_____. Terms: net 30-days.

If there is any discrepancy, please call me at _____. Thank you for your continued patronage.

Sincerely,

_____

Second Letter to Past Due Account

Dear _____:

We have not received payment for our Invoice #_____ in the amount of $_____. Your account is now _____ days past due.

If you are having difficulty, we will work with you if at all possible. It is urgent that you contact me at your earliest opportunity if payment can't be remitted by return mail. An addressed, postage-paid envelope is enclosed for your convenience.

Sincerely,

_____

Third Letter to Past Due Account

Dear _____:

Repeated efforts to cooperate with you have been made since last September to no avail. You have chosen to ignore our attempts to obtain payment on our Invoice #_____ in the amount of $_____.

We now have no choice but to turn your account over to our attorney for possible legal action. This will be done on _____, 19_____, if the invoice is still unpaid on that date. This outcome would be regretted since we feel that everything possible was done by our organization to achieve an agreeable solution.

Sincerely,

_____

Now we'll look at a few hidden expenses that can gobble up profits if you're not aware of how to control them.

RESTOCKING, HANDLING, AND OTHER HIDDEN EXPENSES

Every time you *touch* a product, it costs you. When an item is returned by a customer, you have to devote time to unpacking it and putting it away so it can be sold another day. Then, every minute that product sits on a shelf, the meter runs because it occupies space that you are paying for. To make matters worse, the longer inventory remains unsold, the more stale it becomes. The passage of time alone can cause deterioration.

Another painful situation will arise from time to time: you may occasionally get returns that have been damaged. In the interest of goodwill, you may not want to create an issue with your customer, so you make a full refund. You are out not only the costs of acquiring the sale and delivering the order, but also the amount of the now useless product itself.

The problem of costly dormant inventory can become a major headache when you start getting to the end of a product's useful market life. Sales on a particular item may begin to slip, and you make the decision to replace it with something fresh and new. That almost always results in a small quantity of leftovers.

Too often those "orphans" go into a dark corner where they start eating up valuable storage space, and consequently cash. Your best solution is to *dump your dead excess at close-out prices*. Salvage whatever cash you can. After all, you probably enjoyed months of profitable sales on the item, and the lower margin you are forced to accept for the final lot now can easily be absorbed.

Some mail order operators donate small lots of leftovers to charities and fund-raising programs. Talk to your accountant about tax deductions on these gifts. Larger lots can sometimes be turned into cash at flea markets.

Packages returned by customers have to be opened and the contents inspected carefully. It might help if you could simply put a new label on the still-sealed box and ship it to a new buyer, but there *have* been surprises in returned boxes that you definitely wouldn't want your new customers to receive. Restocking is a cost you have to bear.

Many other common traps to avoid in mail order are now reviewed.

CHAPTER 12

AVOIDING PITFALLS THAT CAN SLOW YOUR GROWTH

Perceptive selections of products and services, good lists, and punchy promotions will not by themselves clinch your long-range success in mail order. There are other vital business and strategy factors that *have to be kept in focus* in order to grow a healthy enterprise.

This chapter covers the common obstacles faced by every mail order operator and describes ways to steer around them.

THE ALL-IMPORTANT TASK OF POSITIONING YOURSELF IN THE INDUSTRY

"Image" is a word that has been used for decades to describe the personality of an individual or business entity. No matter how small your company, it does have—or *should* have—a personality.

This unique identity conveys to consumers a feeling about *how* a firm does business—whether it's cold and businesslike or warm, friendly, and supportive. Those components are transmitted through the look of ads and mailers, the tone of letters and product copy, and attitudes that come across in personal meetings or by telephone.

But the aspect of image we want to address now is the *direction* of a company as perceived by the buying public. Consumers will feel more confidence, and hence will be more apt to purchase, if they feel a merchandiser occupies and is devoted to a *specific market niche*. When you successfully zero in on a clearly defined position, these advantages accrue to you:

- Your prospect base becomes much more definable. This enables you to target your promotions with much more precision. That saves money and enhances results.

- Customers come to identify your company with certain merchandise categories. When a need arises, they know where to look. Equally important, you will eventually be recognized as a specialist in your chosen niche, and that can help tremendously.

- By establishing consistency in the types of products and services you offer, relationships can be built with a more manageable group of suppliers.

- Perhaps most significant of all, your company is seen as an organization that has a definite path and goal. Wide divergences in product selection from one promotion to the next tend to look scattered.

Oddly enough, it's more difficult to *remain* focused on an ongoing basis than to pick and stick with a niche in the start-up stages of an enterprise. Here's how it often works.

REMAINING FOCUSED ON YOUR PRIMARY OBJECTIVES

As a mail order company starts to prosper, unsolicited merchandise opportunities begin to roll in. Success attracts the attention of suppliers who claim to have perfect additions to your line. Suddenly you can slow down your efforts to locate sources because sharp distributors want a ride on your bandwagon. These very flattering offers can be awfully hard to resist.

At these times of temptation, you have to muster the will power to step back and unemotionally appraise every facet of every deal that comes your way. Does it really fit the market position you have carved out for yourself? Would it require the addition of yet other products and facilities you may not want to acquire? Would it create a new commitment of time and money you'd rather avoid?

Charles Reed, owner and operator of a mail order firm selling music system components, made this comment about straying off course:

> "In my ten years in this business, the toughest decision I had to make was about a related product category that could have tripled the scope of my selection. The distributor had put together an outstanding proposal. One part of me said it was the way to grow, and possibly the right time for expansion. Another inner voice kept saying 'consolidate what you are already doing well. Don't get into an area you don't really understand, that would stretch you financially.' I finally resisted making the move, and I've never been sorry about that decision."

A surprisingly large number of small but growing mail order firms succumb to the allure of new products and services and fail as a direct consequence.

When the decision is too close to call, *testing* is recommended. If the new category or item you are considering *is* related to your tried and true product line, you have an absolutely perfect audience to sound out in the form of your current customers. Test results may very well lead you to the right decision. Refer back to Chapter 4 for testing approaches.

While focus on a definite market position is strongly advised for both new and growing mail order companies, the *name* of the company should allow flexibility in future directions you may decide to take.

NAMING YOUR MAIL ORDER COMPANY SO YOU DON'T PAINT YOURSELF INTO A CORNER

When Roy Adams started running media ads in 1968 selling typewriters, he didn't know that by 1975 he'd be exclusively in computers and peripherals and that typewriters would be on the verge of extinction. He originally named his company Troy Typewriter Sales. Paula Bergin put together a mail order lingerie business. Within three years her line was made up entirely of women's athletic outfits. Paula's firm had been christened Bergin Intimates.

Both people freely admit today that their starting formal identities were shortsighted and caused severe inconvenience and needless expense in later years. Reprinting promotional materials, labels, letterheads, and other forms of identity represented only part of the upheaval. Reeducating customers was the biggest worry, along with sustaining name recognition among prospects.

Neither Roy Adams or Paula Bergin made drastic switches to different types of merchandise. They evolved over a period of time into closely related product areas. That sort of gradual transition will take place in a majority of growing mail order companies. For that reason, it is limiting to call a new firm *Scott Glass Ornaments*, *Videotape Storage Systems*, or any other name that becomes a liability when the business changes the character of its products.

Trends can also force business names into obsolescence. For example, does the name *Hi-Fi Systems* evoke images of a firm selling state-of-the-art compact disc equipment? Does a business identity like *Pete's Gym Shoe Warehouse* adequately fit this era of advanced and often costly footwear designed for every imaginable activity?

If at all possible, stay away from any name that clearly describes your present product or category of the moment. Also avoid specific geographical references such as *Route 252 Art Supplies* or *Chicago Heights Linen Importers*. As soon as you move, you'll discover how expensive and disruptive those choices can become.

Trendy names are to be shunned as well. Today's rage *will* become terribly stale in one year or less. In fact, the more intense the craze, the sillier it will look, and the faster it will happen. Can you think of any firm name as tired as one taken from a hot dance step, a popular toy, or a top-rated TV series?

Each mail order firm mentioned here had to be renamed. The new tags work quite well according to the various owners. Some of those new names are:

Troy Business Systems
Bergin ActionWear
Reflections by Scott
SoundPro, Inc.
Competition Shoes

Every one will permit more than enough change of direction in merchandise selection.

Our next pitfall has to do with getting complacent.

KEEPING FRESH NEW IDEAS FLOWING

Whether or not you like its present state, our world moves relentlessly forward. When a certain product or service line is selling with consistent strength, many mail order operators become content to sit on the status quo. While sales may be soaring, the clock is ticking. New, better values are surely on the way, and they will invariably become buyer favorites. That process can take weeks, months, or years. In any case, a mail order operator has to see those changes coming and make the necessary adjustments in time.

Present suppliers often have to be gently prodded by you to search world markets for hot new items since they may also be guilty of resting on their laurels. That's very much a part of the buyer/supplier partnership described earlier in this handbook. In addition, *new* sources should be explored on an ongoing basis by the owner/buyer of any mail order firm.

We are definitely more sophisticated consumers than we were just a few years ago. Many people can merely glance at a catalog and quickly evaluate the freshness and value of the products. So it clearly pays to cast your lot with those aware consumers instead of the dwindling number of people who are unable or unwilling to discern value and style. The future lies with quality.

We'll now turn to a mail order business strategy that can rescue astute mail order company owners from the pitfall of carrying huge, expensive inventory.

ELIMINATING INVENTORY THROUGH DROP SHIPPING

Earl Gills sells highly specialized optical devices by mail. The typical product in his line retails for hundreds of dollars and is extremely sensitive. Shipping an item safely is almost a science in itself.

When Gills first looked into starting his business, he was nearly discouraged at the prospect of buying and stocking a fortune in products. Aside from the enormous cost for stock, he faced the need to create a specially constructed warehouse that was both climate controlled and resistant to shock and fire. An investment that was out of the question in view of his budget.

As a last resort, Gills asked the suppliers he had selected if they would *drop ship* orders to his mail order buyers. In all but one case, the answers were affirmative. The arrangement would work this way:

> When an order came in from a customer, Gills would complete one of his custom-printed mailing labels by printing the customer's name and address. This label would be sent to the supplier, along with a purchase order and payment in full.
>
> The supplier would promptly affix the label provided by Gills and forward the product to the consumer in special protective packaging.

To the customer, the package that arrives looks for all the world as if it was sent from the mail order optical company, thus protecting the buyer/seller relationship. A consumer had absolutely no way of knowing that Earl Gills never had physical possession of the product. It went from the manufacturer *directly* to the mail order customer.

There are a multitude of advantages in drop shipping. In addition to eliminating the need to buy inventory and warehouse it, a mail order company can cut the product's journey from the supplier to the seller's warehouse. In the case of sensitive or fragile products, that reduced handling can go a long way toward controlling loss through breakage.

Drop shipping can work with products that have the following characteristics:

- Exceptionally large size.

- Fragile and/or sensitive products.

- Costly items, since no sane supplier would agree to take on the burden of drop shipping one item worth $6.

- Any service that *has to be* provided from the originator, and where the mail order firm is acting only as the selling agent.

- Last but not least, your supplier has to agree to take you on as a client *without* requiring the purchase of some minimum quantity. Remember, you buy as you go.

There is one potential pitfall in drop shipping, pointed out now.

PROTECTING THE IDENTITY OF YOUR CUSTOMERS

By now you fully realize that your mailing list easily represents your most valuable business asset. In the mail order industry, there is simply no more precious possession. For that reason, some mail order owners adamantly refuse to have suppliers drop ship. They are concerned that people at the supplier level will steal their customers.

If that seems overly paranoid to you, be assured that it *has* happened on more than one occasion. A supplier who is disposed to larceny simply has to record customer names and addresses from the labels sent by a mail order outfit, and presto!, they work themselves into a position to sell directly to active end users.

Stealing customers in this manner is, of course, grossly unethical. And it's extremely rare since an overwhelming majority of suppliers are honest. Besides, most of them want nothing to do with selling direct to end users.

Still, if you look into drop shipping as a viable way to do business, keep that vulnerability in mind, and *question* your would-be suppliers about their security and their attitudes about your valued customers. Above all, let them know that you *are* aware of the peril.

If you ever suspect a supplier of encroaching on your customer base, try this:

> Order a product in the name of a friend or relative (you can always use the product to fill an order). Ask that trusted individual to let you know if *any* offers arrive in their mail box from that particular firm.

Here are some other perils you can easily sidestep to reduce your exposure.

CUTTING DELIVERY RISKS TO THE MINIMUM

Probably the most overused and distorted phrase in commerce is, "The customer is always right." Without question, any company building a reputation for service has to take special and sometimes painful steps to keep buyers happy. But that does *not* mean that sound business principles can be ignored to please consumers.

These items are all related to product and service delivery. Each can turn into a pitfall if neglected in the name of good service.

Extending Credit On Mail Order Purchases

Consumers who regularly send in orders over a long period of time have been known suddenly to request billing, despite a history of paying cash in advance according to the mail order firm's policy.

On occasion, the mail order firm's owner or manager somehow becomes convinced that refusal to grant deferred payment will lose the valued customer. While refusal may indeed kill some of these orders, it is decidedly *more* risky to start entering the credit business. Once the first exception is made, the door is open to a flood of credit transactions—and the serious losses that accompany the granting of credit.

Mail order is a *cash* business. Advice: Politely decline customer requests to pay later.

Filling an Order Before the Customer's Check Clears

Orders are normally covered by money orders, credit cards, and personal checks. Of these, only checks represent a risk, assuming that you properly verify the validity of credit cards.

On very small orders, some mail order operators take their chances and send merchandise prior to bank clearance of funds. They reason that the risk of NFC checks is outweighed by the hassle involved in waiting when only a few dollars are at stake.

Good business practice dictates *waiting* until personal checks clear, regardless of order dollar amount.

COD Transactions

Cash on delivery is definitely *not* a favored payment method in the mail order business. It is occasionally used in business-to-business transactions when high-ticket sales are made, but almost never for typical consumer orders.

If a purchaser is rarely at home, or that consumer changes his or her mind about the order, you will be stuck for delivery and handling expenses. Accepting CODs invites problems.

Importing can be an enormous pitfall for mail order companies. We'll review some of the reasons why.

IMPORT/EXPORT: THE CONSIDERABLE PROS AND CONS

Buying direct from an overseas manufacturer can bring a U.S. based mail order company distinct benefits. But each advantage is shadowed by a serious potential drawback. Some of those drawbacks can be controlled; others cannot. For example:

- By virtue of lower labor costs that often prevail in some other countries, certain imported products stand to be priced very low compared to comparable goods made domestically. But . . .

  many manufacturers in other countries have become sophisticated marketers, so price has to be *negotiated* with them. You can't simply assume that the prices they quote over there are competitive. Another factor to watch out for is the cost of freight which has to be factored into product cost.

- Many overseas manufacturers employ people who can communicate in English. This is essential in working out the myriad details of a transaction. But. . .

  many still do *not* have an English-speaking capability. That makes it necessary for you to deal through an agent who represents one or more factories. This can solve the communications problem, but increases the price you'll pay for the merchandise.

- Obtaining special designs, fashions, colors, and other custom features from overseas factories is a definite possibility since many of them are small enough to be flexible and eager to get U.S. distribution. But . . .

  sudden world crises can instantly and perhaps permanently dry up a product pipeline. In the most drastic circumstances, that break can take place right after a big order has been paid for by a mail order firm.

Also, orders are sometimes received with the wrong products, with many broken items, and short of the requested count. When recourse *is* possible, it could take months to straighten out problems like these.

- Airfreight can bring orders to you much more quickly than over-the-water shipping. And the higher costs are often worthwhile. But . . .

The production schedule of some overseas producers are such that delays of many months are not unusual. Predicting when your merchandise will arrive is still virtually impossible in many instances. That situation puts pressure on the timing of mailings and ads and on your finances since rates of exchange can rise or fall while you're waiting for delivery.

Unless you are in a position to buy in large quantities, negotiate through capable and reputable agents, and take some chances, importing is best avoided by new mail order firms.

A potential pitfall that never fails to cause apprehension is the creative aspect of mail order.

GETTING COPY, ILLUSTRATION, AND DESIGN DONE AT LITTLE OR NO COST

Thousands of people have been discouraged from entering mail order because they lack "artistic" or "creative" ability. Mailer and ad layout, product and service descriptive copy, selection of illustrations and photos, and promotion formats often combine to overwhelm an individual who has never done any of those things.

In truth, this is the *only* attribute important to a successful mail order entrepreneur: The ability to visualize the general appearance of the finished promotion and a sense of what it should convey to the customer.

That's a far cry from possessing the ability to sit down and actually *perform* the artistic and creative steps. You *should* have the instincts to capably supervise the promotion-building process. But skill as a writer or illustrator is about as necessary for you as welding or riveting is for the chairman of an aerospace company.

There are plenty of sources available to you for getting the creative job done. Some will cost money, others will not. Here's a rundown:

Product and Service Copy

Your supplier will invariably have professionally crafted descriptions you can use. If not, this very satisfactory avenue is open to you: Collect copy on items similar to yours found in ads, catalogs, and other sources. Then put together whatever you need from that material. A sharp high school or college student can edit your compilation.

Strive for *simplicity and punch*. The language has to be perfectly clear, easy to read, and as brief as practical.

Figure 12-1 provides a good example of copy that was created from various descriptions used for products similar to the one advertised.

Figure 12-1. Turning Dry Information into Lively Sales Copy

This factory brochure copy for a knife sharpener —

> Presenting the Edge Machine. This device consists of two rods set in a wood platform at 20 degree angles. With just a few vertical strokes on the rods, a sharp new edge is created.

was transformed to this excellent mail order selling copy —

> THERE'S *NO* BLADE THAT THIS SHARPENER CAN'T TURN INTO A RAZOR!
>
> It sharpens serrated blades, curved blades, scissors—even your circular saw blades! And it does all that with the finest hardened rods, set into a seasoned hardwood base.
>
> They're precisely positioned to eliminate worry about keeping your blade at the correct angle. Sharpens both stainless and carbon blades IN UNDER A MINUTE. Touches 'em up in *seconds*.

Illustrations and Photos

Here, again, your supplier will very likely have support for you. Illustrations will be far less costly to print than photos that require special processing for quality reproduction.

In the absence of supplier pictures of any kind, a good number of mail order entrepreneurs use their own homemade photos for mailers, ads, and catalogs. They usually shoot black and white film with the item set up against a white backdrop. Color photos are tricky to work with for one-color printing projects.

Whether you pose your item against a suitable backdrop or not, almost any printer can mechanically drop out the background of your picture, giving you just the product image to be shown in the promotion. Illustrations may be cheaper to print, but they cost considerably more to create if you have to hire an artist to get them done.

A homemade 35mm shot taken against a white background can give you satisfactory results, especially if you do extra work on lighting so shadows are largely eliminated. But even if you do get shadows, your printer can help control the quality.

Most home-based mail order operators will tell you that getting pictures of glass and highly reflective objects can be extremely tricky. One entrepreneur complained about trying to shoot a stainless steel water pitcher. He kept picking up the reflected image of the photographer!

Clear glass can become virtually invisible unless some method is used to make the item almost opaque so the lens can "see" it. One advertiser tried spray-painting the edges of glass pieces a very light gray. It worked beautifully for black and white shots.

Design and Layout

Ideas can come from other promotions you've seen. Find a printing company that has a competent layout department. Check out some of the recent work they've done. If you're pleased with their design approach, give them examples of the "look" you want to achieve. By working with them, you should be able to reach a point of satisfaction.

Most printers will charge extra for design and pre-press composition. Or, if you used an artist to do illustrations, perhaps that person can help with the design task for a little more money.

For ads, the publication staff can almost always assist in doing a nice layout.

Mailer Format

Your best choice is to start with a *proven* format, one that has been successful for one or more other companies. To track down tested formats, watch your own mail carefully. Save mailing examples that are repeated from time to time. You can have more trust in the formats that are used more than once.

By all means avoid reinventing the wheel in the beginning. Start-up is *not* the time to experiment.

Our final pitfall is about your valuable time.

MANAGING YOUR TIME TO MAXIMUM ADVANTAGE

Bev Collins quit her job at a supermarket and started running ads selling hand-painted coffee mugs. By the time her third ad ran, she was at break-even. The outlook was bright. Bev predicted an operating profit in 60 days. Then she ran into problems.

Filling orders became an all-consuming task. At the rate of 30 orders a day, the mug seller's time was almost completely dominated by packing and mailing products, trips to the post office, entering data in the computer, plus scores of other details necessary to getting orders delivered. Locating new designs, searching for other productive media, and developing better ads came to a virtual standstill. In essence, the vital actions that produce revenue had been seriously impaired.

It took Bev Collins almost a month to figure a way out of the downward spiral she was caught in. The answer was to prioritize tasks and then *delegate* the relatively unimportant ones to a competent employee. Bev's level of sales warranted assistance.

A part-time person was hired to process orders, pack and mail products, and track inventory. The improvement was instant and dramatic. Business once again took off, and there was sufficient time for the boss to assure that it remained on that upward course.

A simple way to make certain you are giving your mail order business sufficient time in the right areas is now provided:

- First, make a list of *every* task required to keep your mail order operation running. When that inventory is complete, go to the next step.

- Assign each listed task to yourself or to an employee. Now is the time to *let go* of any pet projects you may enjoy doing, but can easily be taken care of by somebody else. If it can be done by another person, *give it up*!

- As soon as you have a list of things that *must* be handled by you, rate them in terms of urgency. Use a 1 to 3 rating, 1 being of extreme importance. Also rate the tasks you've decided to delegate.

- Now you have a prioritized list of chores for yourself and an employee. You can start working on key tasks immediately. The others can wait a bit.

  When you hire an assistant, you'll be able to make up a schedule for that person that puts first things first.

Prioritizing is absolutely vital if you are attempting to operate a mail order enterprise smoothly in addition to another job. Using this simple system, you'll never get tangled up in chores that can be done more efficiently by a bright and industrious student who can spend a few hours a day with you.

Operating your mail order enterprise from your residence can be a dream come true—*if* you organize it well. The next chapter covers the important aspects of doing that. Also included is a bonus section on the legalities you'll have to be aware of as a direct marketing entrepreneur.

CHAPTER 13

SETTING UP YOUR MAIL ORDER COMPANY AT HOME

According to major surveys, some 10 percent of the U.S. work force now conducts business at home on a full-time basis. By the year 2000, *14 percent* are expected to be operating from their residences. Some of these people are salaried workers who can handle their jobs off-site. But a clear majority will be entrepreneurs who, for a variety of reasons, prefer a home office. You can be certain that lots of them are mail order companies.

In most direct response situations, customers rarely if ever visit the selling company. That being the case, why would any marketer go to the expense of renting and furnishing costly office space? As long as your home mail box can hold the daily flow of orders and your telephone is adequate for inbound calls—a residence can serve the purpose beautifully.

Of course there *are* other important issues to take care of in making your mail order business work successfully from your home. We'll take a look at each of those issues in this chapter.

THE PROS AND CONS OF WORKING AT HOME

Aside from the pure comfort and convenience of conducting business from your residence, there are these compelling reasons to consider:

- Studies show that home workers are *more productive* than their office-bound counterparts. That goes against conventional wisdom, which suggests that lack of supervision leads to less output. The truth is, there are fewer distractions at home and no travel time to contend with. For mature people, the absence of a supervisor doesn't matter in the least in terms of getting the job done.

- Not only do you eliminate rental and utility costs on commercial office space, you also get important tax breaks in a home office. The portion of a residence used for business is deductible. More detail about that is presented later.

There *are* some downside aspects to think about. For example, many home-based workers discover they miss regular contact with other people. Generally speaking, it's a more solitary existence than being in an office environment. For those bothered by the lack of contact, it's vital to make a greater effort to network and establish outside ties. On the other hand, some folks prefer the more isolated style.

Space can be a drawback in a home operation if you don't happen to have a large residence with spare rooms. Small quarters can stretch one's creative utilization of space. Cleverly done, an office by day can be transformed to a family room by night. It isn't always convenient or as pretty as you'd like, but it serves the purpose until larger living facilities become practical.

Another potential drawback is a well-meaning family. Kids and other close relatives may have trouble realizing that worktime to a home operator is every bit as valuable as it is to an office employee. Certain hours of the day are *strictly* for getting tasks accomplished, and those close to you have to understand that. So ground rules regarding interruptions must be firmly set in place.

How should a home-based company present its address? That has been a controversial issue in the past, but isn't quite as tricky today. We'll talk about it now.

HOW TO HANDLE A BUSINESS ADDRESS

Some mail order entrepreneurs feel that home addresses don't sound enough like business addresses, and thus fail to project a professional image. In fact, the only way people will know that your address is in a residential district is if they live in or near your community and know the neighborhood intimately. The distinction is particularly hard to make in this age of comparatively charming suburban industrial parks with street names like Delores Ravine Drive and Sunshine Lane.

The real drawback in using your home address is the propensity of many Americans to move every few years. That can cause big reprinting bills and massive confusion to customers and vendors alike.

Local zoning regulations may also keep you from formally declaring your home address a place of business. While the tremendous popularity of working from home is putting pressure on prohibitions of that nature, you should still find out if you can run a business from your residence.

Due to those considerations, use of a P.O. box is often a very good alternative. Private firms rent mailboxes of all sizes at competitive rates. Better yet, they *do* provide an address for you to use, and it's usually in a commercial neighborhood. The box number can be shown as a suite number, so customers believe the address is indeed an office, not a mere metal box.

Larger post offices rent boxes, as they have done for years. In that case, the designation *P.O. Box 0000* has to be used. So your customer knows you are picking your mail up at a location other than your office. Until rather recently, P.O. boxes were considered unprofessional by purists in the mail order field. They felt that such an address looked temporary, as if the firm were always moving in an effort to remain a step in front of creditors. But today some of the biggest corporations freely use P.O. box numbers, with the result that the argument about trust no longer holds water.

Before we get into the specifics of setting up a home-based mail order business, we'll touch on areas of the field that require some extra care from a legal standpoint.

IMPORTANT LEGAL ISSUES TO BE AWARE OF

Mail order is a field that has earned so many people so much money over so long a period of time, it's certainly not surprising that abuses have occurred—and still do. Some of the scams are so imaginative, one has to wonder why that kind of ingenuity isn't used by mail order operators to make *legitimate* fortunes!

Because of the occasional rip-off attempts, there are certain regulations in force intended to protect consumers. Some of them pertain to cancellation policies, some to the claims a promoter can make, some to the kinds of products that can be sold by mail, and so on.

Mail order operators have to contend not only with federal laws, but also must stay on the right side of the Postal Service—and state attorneys general who would prosecute consumer fraud cases.

This section does not go into specific rules and regulations, but helps to make you aware of what to watch out for and measures to take that can keep you in the clear.

Setting Up Ethical Standards

Most legal hassles can be avoided simply by establishing a code that is based on complete fairness to customers. Such a code of ethics should be spelled out by you in every transaction. Some companies put the text of their ethical code in the form of a guarantee to customers. One good example was provided in Chapter 8 ("Why Guarantees Help Assure Mail Order Success"). Figure 13-1 shows another.

Aside from publicized ethical standards, there are certain operating principles that might be very much a part of how you conduct business, but could remain unpublicized. Here are a few:

- That customers would *never* be challenged with regard to cancellations, price protests, returns, or any other issues like those. These center on the old advice, "The customer is always right."

- That when a refund has to be made, it goes out *immediately*.

Performance and Quality Claims

Exaggerated claims of what a product or service can do will almost surely draw fire at some point and cause you more grief than the extra sales could ever justify. It *is* tempting to go to or beyond the limits in descriptive copy and specifications. But it *does pay* to take a safer,

Ken Nolan's *NO-RISK GUARANTEE*

YOU CAN BUY WITH CONFIDENCE. If ever you are not satisfied with anything you bought from us you may return it complete and in original condition within 30 days for a prompt exchange, adjustment or refund. Be sure to wrap securely and insure the merchandise. Include a note detailing the NATURE OF THE PROBLEM, NAME & DATE ON ORIGINAL, METHOD OF PAYMENT AND WHAT YOU WANT US TO DO. Custom, special order and personalized items may be returned if your written instructions were not followed.

Ken Nolan Customer Service (714) 863-1532
16901 Milliken – Irvine, CA 92713-9555

Figure 13-1. A Good Customer Assurance Guarantee

more conservative approach in your copy. It is also risky to put a product of yours on even terms with a competitive version that's top of the line, of high repute, and much more costly.

Federal Regulations

Laws govern certain aspects of mail order. People who purchase a product or service sight unseen are protected to some extent. Some of those laws cover:

- Conforming to a customer or prospect's demand for you to stop mailing. When you receive a request to cease all future mailings, you have to do so according to the regulations.

- Accepting cancellations and the resulting returned merchandise and then granting prompt refunds, within a reasonable length of time after the original purchase. More than a few mail order operators have been in hot water over this one.

- Delivering customer orders promptly. The law spells out how quickly you have to send out merchandise or begin rendering the purchased service.

To get the *very latest* legal guidelines for mail order operations, contact this organization:

Direct Marketing Association
11 West 42nd Street
New York, NY 10036
(212) 768-7277

If you live in or near a sizable metropolitan area, you may find a local direct marketing association that can be tremendously helpful.

Now more specifics about what you need to conduct business from your residence.

SETTING UP A COMFORTABLE, EFFICIENT HOME OFFICE

Your objective is to turn your residence into a completely functional place of business *without* reducing your quality of life in any way.

You want to retain the warmth and comfort of your environment, but still have whatever you need to conduct operations.

Administrative aspects of mail order, such as buying, correspondence, bill paying, and similar functions, can be handled at a desk. This area should look like practically any other desk in almost any residence. It includes files, perhaps a computer, and the usual office items. Figure 13-2 shows a typical administrative center. This particular one is in one corner of a living room and fits in beautifully with the other room decor.

Figure 13-2. An Administrative Center That Fits in a Living Room or Den

Order processing aspects of your mail order enterprise might require a bit more resourcefulness on your part. You'll need a fairly large and sturdy work surface suitable for packing and unpacking products. Very close to your work surface, you must have easy access to rolls of wrapping paper, sealing tape, rolls of twine, and everything else required to get outgoing orders ready.

Nearby, you'll have cardboard shipping cartons, stored flat to conserve important space. Whatever product inventory you stock will also be very close at hand. A strong metal shelving system, available in kit form at any good hardware or industrial supply store can serve for storage.

Your order processing area is best set up in a spare bedroom, a garage, or a basement. Figure 13-3 illustrates a typical order processing layout.

Figure 13-3. One Example of an Order Processing Center

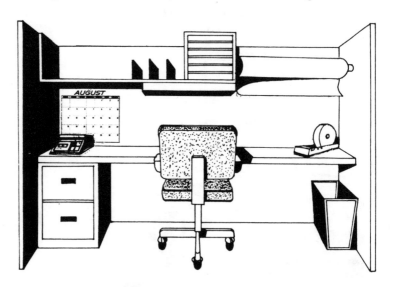

In setting up a processing area, these important items should be covered:

- Try to cut the *distance* items have to travel from one step to the next. You want to be able to grab a product, package it, and then take it to a mailing pickup point and do all of that in the most compact space possible. That saves considerable time and effort.

- If you decide to utilize a basement or garage for processing orders and storing inventory, make absolutely sure that cold, dampness, or other adverse conditions can't ruin your stock or your costly packing materials. Also, be certain that *you* will be comfortable during those times of preparing orders.

- Take care that your processing center is just as secure as your administrative area.

More detail now on getting orders ready to ship.

TIPS ON PACKAGING ORDERS

Once you have decided on the products you'll offer, you can start working out the best possible system for preparing those items for mailing. Your basic goals should be:

- To *standardize* the packing procedure as much as possible. For example, can you get by with one box size instead of two or more? Can the same type of packing material be used for all products? Keep it as simple as you can.

- Will your most fragile items ride safely en route to customers? Take whatever precautions are necessary to avoid breakage.

- Have you shopped for the best prices on packing materials? These items can cost a fortune if you buy them retail. You *have to* find sources willing to work with you at favorable rates.

To get valuable help on *how* to package, visit a few packaging stores and ask them questions. Most larger cities have shops like these, and they can assist you in working out a system that makes sense.

Before you make a commitment to buy large quantities to get better prices on cartons, tape, and other packaging components, read the next sections.

IDEAS FOR KEEPING NEEDED SUPPLIES
UNDER CONTROL

In negotiating prices for office and packaging supplies, it's easy to get price breaks when you agree to take delivery of large quantities. But operating from home restricts your ability to stock, say, 500 cartons or 72 rolls of sealing tape.

You have to strike a deal that enables you to make a commitment to purchase substantial quantities *over a period of time*. An arrangement like that lets you take delivery on just the quantities you need for a couple of weeks. You want a supplier who is willing to give you a quantity price break, but is open to letting you use *its* warehouse.

One packaging material supplier in Texas is agreeable to warehousing for smaller clients *if* the purchaser contracts to buy in quantity for the coming year, and if the purchaser will *pick up* needed supplies. Eliminating delivery makes the difference for this packaging distributor.

Here's another way to conserve scarce residential space.

ARRANGING FOR DAILY PICKUPS OF OUTBOUND ORDERS

When you have 40 customer orders ready to go—and that mountain of boxes blocks your front door—you'll realize the urgency of getting *daily* pickup service. Unless you happen to have a truck of your own, you'll definitely want to avoid the chore of taking those customer orders to the post office, UPS, or other delivery service. By all means, let *them* stop by with their truck at a prearranged daily time. It will prevent those stacks of boxes from growing out of control and will certainly save lots of your valuable time.

When you set up a standing daily pickup time, you are a regular customer. As such, many delivery services will be able to simplify the system for you. That will save you even more time on clerical entries.

Some home-based mail order operators arrange to *receive* packages via the same service they use for delivering orders. That means one less truck in your driveway, thus less irritation to sensitive neighbors. Also, you'll get generally better service because a relationship exists with the driver who is often a regular on the route. The more business you do with one delivery outfit, the more you'll receive in special care when you need it.

Now, here is another tip on space saving.

HOW TO STORE RECORDS WHEN THERE'S NO ROOM

You may discover that remote storage facilities offer a great opportunity to save space in your home. If you are trying to operate in a small area, the availability of a big self-storage room can save the day.

Use an outside rental storage area for:

- Records that no longer have to be accessed regularly. That includes invoices, correspondence, etc.

- Certain products, especially when you have a sudden influx of items you have purchased or you receive a flood of samples you have to review.

- Packaging supplies, if you are unable to work out warehousing by your supplier.

If you are faced with conducting business from extremely cramped home facilities, shop for a storage room that provides the features you need. They can be heated, secure, ventilated, equipped with sprinklers, the right size for your needs, accessible 24 hours, open seven days a week, convenient to where you live, and so forth.

An array of technological developments have given home business operators the communications tools needed to stay in touch with their customers, prospects, and suppliers. We'll cover those interesting areas now.

EASY-TO-USE ELECTRONIC TOOLS
FOR HOME BUSINESSES

As you continue in your home mail order business, you'll discover that certain electronic wonders will help you operate much more effectively. Most of these devices don't cost a fortune, but provide extremely valuable service. Here's a look at the most important ones:

Voice mail is simply an elaborate version of the old answering machine. The difference is, if the person calling you has a touchtone phone, he or she can punch certain numbers and receive recorded information, get connected with various departments, or leave messages if desired. For example, after the system answers, it can prompt the caller like this:

"If you'd like to place an order, please press 1."

"If you want service, press 2."

"If you know the extension number of the person you'd like to talk to, please press 3."

"For all other needs, please press 4."

If you'll be taking orders by telephone, an approach like this can be invaluable. But not everybody loves these systems. Judith Blake, a staff reporter for the Seattle *Times*, said this about voice mail:

> You can call it technology. Or torture by telephone. It saves time. It wastes time. It's efficient. It's maddening. It's voice mail.

Critics complain mostly about the lack of human contact. But for busy inbound lines carrying a high volume of orders, voice mail can do a lot more good than harm. For example, one magazine has a system that can "converse" with subscribers. A recorded voice asks you to "fill in" audio blanks with name, address. The entire sale is automated.

Personal computers have been mentioned earlier in this book. If you've been resisting the concept of data processing, consider the applications you can use a computer for in a home enterprise. A few of the major ones are:

- Developing customer, prospect, and vendor correspondence. In addition, you could gain the capability of communicating with *other* computers via a modem that permits use of phone lines so computers can "talk" to each other. That's particularly useful in dealing with suppliers.

- Controlling inventory. You could easily do daily stock updates on a simple machine.

- Assigning virtually all bookkeeping functions, including billing and financial reports.

- Maintaining prospect and customer lists and printing of mailing labels.

Having a computer with the right software is very much like having a valued employee at your service. Consult a reputable computer dealer for advice on the best equipment choices for your needs. Don't overbuy! At the same time, consider your growth down the road, and what it will take to keep up with the larger demands you'll encounter later. Get more than one expert opinion before you buy.

Next, consider a computer that does highly specialized tasks.

Desktop publishing takes the computer to marvelous new levels. This extraordinary software seems to be designed for mail order companies since it can essentially handle the composition of newsletters, flyers, and almost any other kind of promotional piece. Desktop publishing capability can virtually eliminate the need to go outside for typesetting, layout, and camera-ready board art. It can do all that.

There *is* a downside: Desktop publishing systems are still pricey. Another factor is skill level. The system will produce work only as good as the operator. Still, at some point in your firm's growth, it could very well pay to look at your cash outlays for outside help and then compare those numbers with the cost of developing your own publishing capability.

Autodialers are used for high-volume outbound telemarketing. They do exactly what the name suggests. You can load many telephone numbers into the system, and it automatically rings the numbers, one after another, until somebody answers. A telemarketer stands by and gets on the line only when a prospect picks up on the other end.

If you plan to conduct a massive *consumer* direct sales program by telephone, an autodialer can increase efficiency. This device produces no benefits for business-to-business calling since a receptionist can always be counted on to pick up your sales call.

Fax machines are very valuable if you have extremely heavy business with vendors or if your customers are companies that also have fax units. But they are difficult to justify when you deal mainly with consumers who probably don't have fax machines. One distinct benefit in fax machines is that they can also make copies.

Our Internal Revenue Service provides clear advantages to home-based entrepreneurs. Here's more information about that.

TAX LAWS YOU CAN USE TO YOUR ADVANTAGE

While pressure is constantly exerted to reduce the tax breaks given to home business operators, the steady growth in the number of people working at home should help assure that many advantages *will* continue for years to come. Some of the breaks traditionally given are:

- You can deduct the rent for that portion of your residence which is used for business.

- Utility costs can be partially deducted in the same way as rent.

- Other expenses, such as insurance and auto expenses, can qualify under certain conditions.

As you may imagine, there have been numerous instances where such deductions have been challenged by the IRS. So it is extremely important for you to do two things before you submit your tax return: (1) Get the opinion of a tax specialist who is totally up to date on current regulations, and (2) take a conservative approach. For example:

> You spend 50 percent of your working time in a spare room to handle order processing, and you use an estimated 40 percent of that room for storing quilts, cameras, etc. But your in-laws visit twice a year for a couple of weeks and sleep there—plus junior uses that space to build model airplanes. So the equation can be tricky and does demand careful reckoning.

Even a conservative calculation will put you far ahead of your acquaintances who work in offices and search desperately for any deductions they can find.

As a home-based mail order entrepreneur, you'll be entering a life of significant challenges, but potentially enormous financial rewards. You will be insulated from the mainstream of humanity, but into a life-style of unprecedented freedom and comfort.

POWERFUL TRENDS EXPECTED TO HELP SMALL MAIL ORDER BUSINESSES

Mailing expenses are climbing steadily upward, and not too many mail order pros believe the escalation will stop anytime soon. That development can do nothing but *boost results for smaller mail order operations.* Here's why:

> Cost-cutting among the industry giants puts a small mailer on more of a level playing field with those big firms. An entrepreneur's modest budget suddenly starts to compete on equal terms with previously big spenders who now find themselves on tight budgets.

Shelby Gilje writes a column called "Troubleshooter" for the Seattle *Times*. She recently pointed out how some of the big, well-heeled mail order houses are taking dramatic steps to get their costs under control. For example,

- Some top firms are charging for delivery for the first time ever.

- Several companies have reduced the size of their catalogs to shave production and mailing costs.

- One of the nation's largest mailers just trimmed 18 million marginal customers from its mailing list of 148 million.

251

- A few major players are testing condensed catalogs that show only the best sellers in their line.

- Pieces previously sent first-class are more often going via third-class to save money.

Perhaps the most interesting trend is renewed interest in *private delivery services*. These firms are in the business of delivering catalogs and other promotions by hanging them on consumer or business doorknobs. That approach steers clear of the heavy traffic in mailboxes and tends to give the advertiser's message more visibility. One of those alternative delivery firms told me that more and more mail order firms are inquiring about private delivery, and some are already testing it.

We urge *you* to explore each of these economy measures.

It looks as if the tremendous power of the huge mail order firms is showing serious cracks. That opens the door even wider for startup mail order companies with comparatively modest money to spend on developing and delivering promotions. The future for small operators in the mail order field looks very bright indeed.

INDEX